How To Get Kids To Do What You Want!

How To Get Kids To Do What You Want!

The Power & Promise of Solution-Focused Parenting

Bill Crawford, Ph.D.

Bill Crawford, Ph.D.
1306 Devon Glen
832-722-6147
1-888-530-8550
DrBill@billcphd.com
www.billcphd.com

To Georgia,
Christopher, &
Nicholas
with all my love

Acknowledgments

As I sit here putting the finishing touches on the third revision of my third book, I am once again amazed at how important the people in one's life can be to the completion of a project such as this. This is especially the case with this book because the subject matter (kids, parenting, etc.) hits so close to home. For that reason, I am grateful that I have the opportunity to thank those who have been such an intregal part in the creation and completion of this work.

Of course, with a book on parenting I must begin by acknowledging my partner in parenting and my partner in life, my wife Georgia. Before meeting her and seeing how she understood and treasured children in such a special way, I had pretty much decided that parenting just wasn't for me. Now of course, I can't imagine life without my two boys, Christopher and Nicholas, and I attribute this change in heart (or maybe just the uncovering of one) to Georgia and her profound love of children.

This love is demonstrated daily as she patiently and enthusiastically interacts with our children in ways that define the role of mother in the most meaningful way I can imagine.

Of course, for a couple to become an effective parental unit, they must share not only a vision for what the process of parenting is all about, but also a common belief in the best way to bring this vision to life. This is certainly the case with our family, and I am pleased to have this opportunity to express my deep and profound appreciation to Georgia, for her contributions to both this book (she could easily be a coauthor) and whatever success we have had and will have as parents.

Of course, you can't be a parent without children, and therefore I must also thank my two sons, Christopher and Nicholas, for giving Georgia and I so many opportunities to "practice what we preach." In addition to providing "grist for the mill," however, they also continue to remind me of the wonders of childhood and how important it is to play and dream, and live as if joy is your highest purpose. When the challenges of adulthood seem to obscure this profound truth, Christopher and Nicholas are always there to remind me of what is really important. Their pictures adorn the cover, and their souls have inspired many of the concepts that make up this book. Thanks, guys!

Finally, no book on parenting would be either possible or complete if there were not an acknowledgment of the parents that allowed Georgia and myself to come into being and eventually come together to create this family and this book.

As I have mentioned in this section of my

first two books, I certainly owe much of who I am and what I believe to my parents, Florence and Burton Crawford.

Although deceased, they continue to inspire not because they were perfect, but because they interacted with me in such a way that their love for me was something I never questioned. I'm sure that having their first child after twenty five years of marriage was quite a shock. However, they brought their love of life and their consistent desire to nurture to their role as parents and for this I will be eternally grateful.

The "parents" that I have had the pleasure of interacting with over the past 25 years are Georgia's mother and father, Effie Rombakis and Dr. Socrates Rombakis, or as our family refers to them, "Yia Yia and Papoo." In my segment on the oxymoron of "grown children," I speak to how important it is for parents to allow their relationships with their children to change as they become adults, and Dr. and Mrs. Rombakis (or "Ma and Dad" as they have encouraged me to think of them) certainly model this as they consistently offered support but not interference in their role as loving grandparents to our children, and mother and father to Georgia.

As I begin my second revision of this work, Dr. Rombakis (Papoo) has passed away and we have the pleasure of sharing a home with Georgia's mother, Effie (Yia Yia). We are thus continually blessed by the daily interaction with our last surviving "parent" and my hope is that Christopher and Nicholas will continue to be served by our love as Georgia and I have been served by the efforts of our parents before us. Thank you for all that you have done, and continue to do. Your legacy is reflected in every word of this book.

Contents

Part I

Part II

Introduction

What is "solution-focused" parenting, and how can it help you get your kids to do what you want? In other words, why should you read this book? The purpose of this book is simply to help you become more powerful and influential in the life of your child. Sound appealing? The approach, which I call "solution-focused parenting" is designed to help you focus your time and energy on teaching your kids what you want them to learn. Also, in addition to helping you conserve and best utilize your time and energy, the solution-focused approach is also designed to minimize your child's resistance to hearing and learning from what you have to say. Easier said than done, right? Right. This isn't about a "miracle cure" or "magic potion" that will turn your kids into little beings that hang on your every word, and live to do your bidding. It is simply a model for interacting with them in a way that 1) Keeps you from getting caught in a power struggle that puts you at odds with your children, 2) Shows you how to tap into your children's internal motivation to hear what you have to say as valuable, and 3) Reinforces the values and qualities that you want them to have as adults.

Before we get into these concepts too deeply, however, let me say a word or two about the population for whom this book is written. While I have great sympathy for parents of kids who have fallen into gangs, hard drugs, and/or trouble with the police, I will not insult these parents' intelligence by suggesting that a simple change in the way they interact with their children will turn the situation around. It's not that I don't believe that the concepts we will discuss in this book could be helpful, it's just that in situations where there are serious problems such as these, I believe a more intense form of intervention will be required first.

Of course, being a psychologist, I have a belief that a mental health professional who has the training and experience to handle this type of problem is the best person to initiate this intervention. The reason I suggest that parents whose kids are in serious trouble enlist the aid of a qualified third party is because it takes the parents out of the power struggle, and gives them some support in re-establishing their role as a guide in their children's lives. Then, once the more serious problems have been dealt with, I believe that the concepts in this book can go a long way to establishing the sort of relationship where children actually hear what their parents are saying, and even look to them for help and guidance.

Also, let me say a word about how this book fits with other books I have written in terms of sequence and content. Prior to writing ***"How to Get Kids To Do What You Want!"*** I have had the pleasure of creating two previous works. They are entitled ***All Stressed Up & Nowhere To Go!*** and ***From Chaos to Calm: Dealing with Difficult People Versus Them Dealing with You!*** Although each of these books deal with different topics (stress and conflict resolution), they *can* be read as a series where each book builds on the next. Also, as you might imagine, "getting kids to do what we want" can be both stressful and conflicted at times, and so I have injected some of the models introduced in the two previous works into this book. In fact, there is a model that I use in all my work, whether counseling individually with clients, or consulting for a Fortune 500 firm, that I believe helps us become more influential in all of our interactions (as well as our life, in general). I have, therefore, also used this model as a basis for this book on ***How to Get Kids to Do What You Want.***

For those of you who have already read any of my previous works, my hope is that this helps you tie the material from all the books together, and enhances your ability to be influential in your children's lives. For those of you who have not read any of my previous works, I have written this book so that it stands alone. Again, my purpose is to both create a series of books that can be read as such, and to write each book so that it can be read without reference to any other work.

Finally, while I have tried to discuss the subject of dealing with children in as complete a way as possible, my guess is that, even after reading this book, you may have questions. If so, please feel free to write me or email me and I will be happy to give you my best thoughts, knowing, of course, that you are the "expert" in the life of your child, and that you will take whatever I say and translate it into your own unique style of teaching and parenting.

Before you begin reading, please list the qualities and/or characteristics you want your child to have when they become an adult:

___

___

___

___

___

___

___

___

___

___

Part I

Chapter 1

Is This A Trick?

How To Get Kids To Do What You Want! Did the title grab you? It certainly does most people. Rest assured, however, this is not just some trick to get your attention. As I have said in the introduction, **my goal, and the goal of this book is to help you become more powerful and influential in the lives of your children**. Whether you are a parent, teacher, uncle, aunt, grandparent or guardian, I believe that you have a tremendous amount of wisdom and life experience that your children desperately need. The problem for most of us is that often our children seem less than enthusiastic about hearing our suggestions and directives as the wisdom and valuable information that it is.

As the parents of two boys, Christopher, age eighteen, and Nicholas age fourteen , my wife, Georgia and I have experienced this frustration first hand. Before putting this method into practice, Georgia and I were always trying to get our boys to either listen, cooperate, play nicely, pick up after themselves, stop whining, stop fighting, get dressed, get undressed, brush their teeth, go to bed, etc. Further, even though they were (and still are) good kids, they just didn't seem to get it! In fact, the more we insisted that they do what we wanted, the more difficult and resistant they became. This, of course, had us becoming more frustrated, insistent, and angry while they became more resistant, resentful, and stubborn!

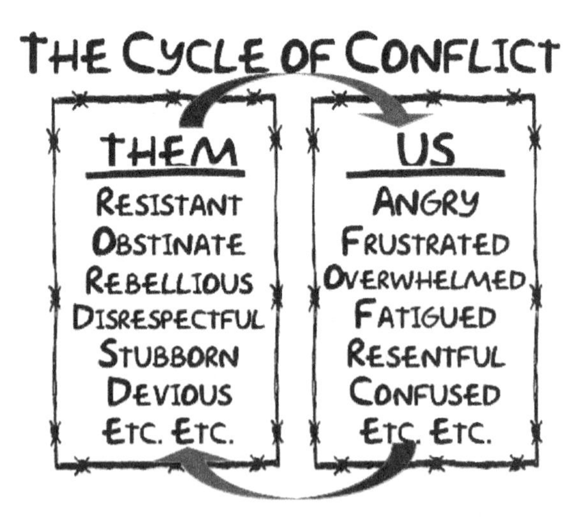

This power struggle, or *Cycle of Conflict* continued until we became so exasperated that we either gave up, or took whatever measures necessary to physically make them obey us! In either case, the result was rarely satisfying. Sound familiar? If so, this book is for you. It is designed to help you get your kids to do what you want, which, ultimately, will be a benefit to your children, as well as, yourself.

What Do We Want?

In becoming skillful at getting our children to do what we want, we must first become very clear about two things: What we really do want, and what we don't. I think we can agree that for all the reasons listed above, the power struggle, or the Cycle of Conflict, is an excellent example of what we don't want (i.e. we feel bad, they feel bad, they stop listening, we don't get the cooperation we're seeking, etc.). If so, this is a great place to start because it can help us avoid falling into that pattern which, for most of us, is all too familiar, uncomfortable, and unproductive. In fact, if all you get from this book is the ability to avoid the power struggle, I believe it will have been worth your time. However, this book is about much more than just avoiding the problem. It's about creating a purposeful and powerful solution.

How do we do that? First, we look at what we do want. On one level, of course, this means what we want them to do, or the behavior that we want them to start or stop, (i.e. pick up their toys, stop whining, stop fighting, get dressed, get undressed, brush their teeth, go to bed, etc.). Getting our children to do these things is certainly important, however, have you noticed that when we focus on *just* getting our children to obey our commands, or perform these behaviors, the result is often resistance? I would like to suggest that there is a more effective way for you to be influential in your children's lives. This method focuses on a higher level of teaching and parenting, a level that actually maximizes our influence, minimizes their resistance, and even taps into their internal motivation to cooperate.

The Power of Purpose

In the model I have developed, becoming clear about what we want really means first becoming very clear about our "purpose" as a parent. Given that any time we are interacting with a child we are teaching them something, becoming clear about what we want, or our purpose, really means becoming clear about what we want to teach. The good news is that you have already done that! If you filled in the blanks on page xii (the characteristics you want your child to have when they become an adult), you have, in a sense, outlined your purpose, for these are the qualities you want your children to learn as a result of your parenting. Or, put another way, this is how you want your children to "turn out" as adults. These qualities and/or characteristics are going to be very important in the following section, so, if for some reason you have not filled in these blanks, please take a moment and do so now.

Raising Adults

If you are like most parents, you probably wrote down such adjectives as intelligent, responsible, honest, compassionate, successful, trustworthy, able to make their own decisions, kind, high self-esteem, etc. All great qualities, to be sure. In fact, as I have traveled around the nation giving workshops on this topic, I have discovered that when asked this question, parents and teachers seem to have very similar responses.

What has really surprised me, however, is not so much what people have said (for, after all, who wouldn't want their children to grow up to be adults with such admirable qualities?). What has really surprised me is what they *haven't* said! Believe it or not, in my many years of asking participants what kind of people they want their children to be when they grow up, no parent or teacher has ever said the word "obedient!"

Of course, this doesn't mean that they don't want their children to grow up to be law-abiding citizens. I'm sure they do. In fact, I would predict that most of us see ourselves as law-abiding citizens, and want this for our kids. However, isn't it a fact that we as adults *choose* the laws we obey? For example, have you ever driven faster than 55 miles per hour? In fact, I would venture to guess that even when we are choosing to obey the laws of our city, state, or nation, most of us don't see ourselves as being "obedient" so much as responsible, honest, cooperative, a good citizen, just as we would want our children to be. And yet, how much time do we spend as parents and teachers teaching our children to be obedient? It's almost like we want them to obey us until they become adults, and then all of a sudden begin thinking and responding as independent individuals who make their own choices and trust their own decisions.

Further, this focus on obedience would be

one thing if it worked well. That is if, as a result of our teaching obedience, our children saw the value in this lesson and became more cooperative, and open to our directives, that would be great! However, have you noticed that often the result is just the opposite? For example, have you noticed that when we are trying to force our children to obey, this is the time they seem to become the most resistant? Remember the power struggle and the Cycle of Conflict?

Suffice it to say, this isn't working. It's not working for us because we find ourselves feeling stressed, exasperated, frustrated, and/or angry as a result of this type of encounter. It's also not working for our children, even if they "win." For example, if their "winning" means they wear us down with their obstinate behavior, tears, or trickery, they learn that the way to get what they want in life is to be obnoxious or pitiful. Not a good lesson. On the other hand, if *we* "win," meaning we are able to force them to obey us, then they feel like they've lost, and are likely to feel less confident in themselves and maybe even resentful of our authority. What we have unwittingly produced is a lesson in powerlessness and resentment, versus responsibility, honesty, and confidence. Further, this often lays a foundation for even more resentment in the future.

Another lesson that we may be unwittingly teaching is the value of avoiding "getting caught" and being "corrected". This may not only have our kids becoming very skilled at "not getting caught" (i.e. how to be sneaky in getting what you want) it may have our children seeing our "correcting them" as punishment, which means that they are not likely to hear our correction as valuable information.

Further, I believe our focus on "raising kids" is another aspect of the situation that may not be working for us. In fact, I'm going to suggest that we are no more raising kids than a chicken farmer is raising chicks, or a cattle rancher is raising calves. In each of these examples the farmer or rancher is focused on their ultimate goal, and this allows them to make choices congruent with their ultimate success. Unfortunately, as parents, our focus is often less on who we want our kids to become and more on what we want them to do now. Therefore, our choices tend to be more how to get them to obey us versus teaching them a quality or characteristic that is congruent with who we want them to be as adults. Given that this isn't working for us or our children, I'm going to suggest that we stop trying to "raise kids" and focus on our ultimate goal which is to produce healthy, happy adults.

So, what does all this mean? Am I saying that we should just let children do whatever they want and never teach them respect for authority? No! Remember what I said earlier? **My purpose, and the purpose of this book is to help you become <u>more</u> powerful and influential in the lives of your children**. I believe they *need* your wisdom and guidance. I believe that they *need* structure, boundaries, and limits. I just want to help you teach these lessons and create these boundaries in a way that reflects the values and qualities you want them to possess as adults. This will keep us (as parents) from lecturing our children to teach them to listen, hurting them to teach them not to hurt others, and yelling at them to teach them not to yell.

The bottom line is that I want to help you practice what you preach so that your words will have more meaning, and your children will see you as an example of the person you want them to become. Or as H. Jackson Brown put it:

"Live your life so that when your children think of fairness, integrity, and caring, they think of you"

H. Jackson Brown

I also want to help you connect with your children in a way that has them hearing your advice and suggestions as the valuable information it is. Finally, I want to give you a method of interacting with your kids in a way that avoids the power struggle, and has them actively participating in the lesson versus resisting and resenting you as the teacher.

In order to achieve this sort of mastery as a parent, I believe we must first understand what is really going on when we find ourselves caught in the "Cycle of Conflict," both in terms of ourselves and our children. This understanding comes from my fourth book, "Life from the Top of the Mind," and I believe goes a long way to differentiating my approach to successful parenting from other experts in the field.

For example, thanks to recent brain research, we now know that when people are frustrated, angry, defensive, or resentful (them or us) it means that the lower 20 % of the brain has been engaged, and that we/they are often responding in a fight-or-flight manner. While this is understandable, it also explains why, as parents, we often find ourselves saying things we never dreamed we would say, and why our kids become resistant to what we are trying to get them to do. *One, or both of us are stuck in the resistant part of the brain and therefore, the only choices we have are fight (where we and/or they become angry, resentful, stubborn, or insistent) or flight (where we and/or they become sad, withdrawn, depressed, or defeated).*

I explain this lower brain reaction in great detail in "Life from the Top of the Mind," however, given that it is such an important piece of the puzzle, I will give you a quick overview here. Basically, as the graphic below shows, our brain is divided into three parts, the brainstem, the limbic system and the neocortex.

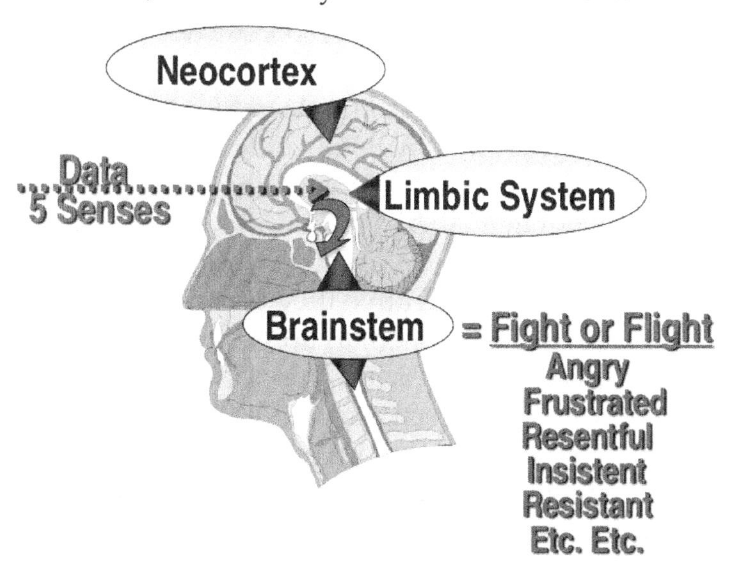

When the data we receive from our five senses is interpreted by our limbic system as negative, problematic or threatening in any way, the brainstem, or the lower 20% of our brain is engaged, and we go into either fight -or-flight, or some combination of the two.

This means that whenever we experience our children being resistant, stubborn, or uncooperative . . . or whenever our kids experience us as being insistent, angry, or demanding, one or both of us are thrown in to the part of the brain that is incapable of solving the problem! Further, when we and our children continue to relate to each other from this lower brain, we create the "cycle of conflict," or the power struggle described earlier in this chapter.

Suffice it to say, unless we as parents can break this cycle and shift to the upper 80 % of our brain where we have access to our higher-order thinking, interpersonal skills, and problem-solving skills, we will never become the type of parents we want to be and our children need.

First we must become clear about our highest purpose as parents, which I'm going to suggest is less about what we want our kids to do, and more about who we want them to be. (Of course, what is fascinating is that the more we focus on who we want them to be, the more cooperative they become in terms of doing what we want them to do.

As mentioned earlier, this not only pertains to *what* you want to teach, but more importantly, *how* you want to teach it, because as I'm sure you have noticed, while **our children don't always do what we say, sooner or later, they will do what we do!**

Becoming clear about your highest purpose,

therefore, means creating a vision of how you would be interacting with, or teaching your children, if you were doing it "on purpose". Given that any time we are interacting with our children we are teaching them something, I would suggest that these "qualities of interaction" be congruent with the qualities you want them to have as adults so that they are learning about how to interact with people by observing how you interact with them.

This is an important first step because the clearer we are about how we want to think, feel, and behave as we interact with (or teach) our children, the more likely we are to be coming from the upper 80% of our mind, and thus the more likely we are to succeed.

Shifting from the Problem to the Solution

Another positive aspect of this parenting style is that in addition to reinforcing the qualities we want to teach, this more purposeful way of being with our children will also have us focusing on the "solution" versus the "problem." While on the surface this might not seem that significant, it is my belief that this shift in focus (from the problem to the solution) can play a huge role in the ultimate success of this endeavor.

Let's take an example from real life. Let's assume that little Johnny just grabbed a toy away from his younger brother (Billy) and made him cry. We, as parents, saw this and immediately jumped in with *"Johnny! What's wrong with you? You know better than that! How would you like it if someone came up to you and grabbed something away from you?"* Now, you might have said it differently, but what most parents would be trying to achieve here was to have little Johnny feel bad about what he did, and stop being mean to his brother, right?

However, have you noticed that when we are trying to get our children to learn a lesson by trying to make them feel bad about "what they did wrong" they seem to want to do everything *but* listen? They may react by arguing, tuning out, defending themselves, looking for someone else to blame, trying to change the subject, making a joke, running and hiding, almost anything to avoid hearing you tell them how they "did it wrong."

There are all sorts of reasons for this, but the bottom line is . . . "THIS ISN'T WORKING!!!!! In other words, this frustrating interaction isn't supporting you in getting your children to do/be what you want, and it may even be laying the foundation for them to tune you out even more in the future.

One of the reasons this focus on "the problem," and our desire to have them "feel bad" about what they did isn't working is because children (especially up to around age 11) are "egocentric". This means that they have trouble separating what they do from who they are. Therefore, when they hear us say that they have done something bad, they hear that "they are bad" and naturally resist seeing themselves this way. This then has them resisting hearing our correction or advice as valuable and thus the power struggle is born.

What can we do? Well first, I'm going to suggest that their feeling "wrong" or "bad" isn't really what we are wanting to achieve. Wouldn't it be fair to say that what we *really* want is for our children to change their behavior in such a way that they would respond differently *in the future?* If so, let's focus on the time frame we are trying to influence (the future) and let's focus on what we are trying to create, a solution, versus just a bad feeling about, or avoidance of, "the problem".

This might have us saying something like: *"Johnny, I noticed that you took a toy from Billy, were you wanting to play with it?*

Knowing that something is up, he might tentatively say: *Yeah.*

To which we might reply: *Well, you know, in our family, when we want something that someone has, we ask them.* (family value reinforced) *Kind of like the other day when I asked if I could use your pen. Do you remember?*

Yeah.

So, next time you want to play with something Billy has what could you do?

To which he might respond with: *Ask him?*

And we might say: *Yes, I am very impressed with how quickly you learn! I tell you what, if I ever forget to ask you when I want something you have, will you remind me of our family rule?*

To which he might say: *Sure will!* (Kids love to be put in the role of teaching their parents!)

You might then say: *Great! If you like, we can ask Billy how long he wants to play with his toy and then you can play with it. We could even set the buzzer so that you know when it's your turn. Okay?*

Now remember, you might have done this very differently. My goal here is not to tell you the exact words to use to deal with a particular incident. Instead, my goal is to introduce the concept of focusing on the solution versus the problem (Top of the Mind versus brainstem) and suggest how this change in focus may be more effective in getting our children to do what we want. Not only does this "teach by example" method give us an opportunity to model the lessons we want them to learn, it reduces their resistance to learning this lesson because we are not trying to get our children to feel bad as a motivation to change.

Put another way, we are not driving them deeper into the reactive, resistant part of their brain nor are we trying to use our anger and frustration as a motivation to teach responsibility and cooperation. Instead we are accessing our higher order thinking and allowing our children to shift to the upper 80% of their brain by focusing on the future and the solution versus the problem and the past. Plus, we are teaching them how to become influential with others in a way we would like them to adopt as adults.

Of course, if you ask most people whether it's a good idea to teach by example, I'm sure you will very likely get a resounding "Yes!" So, if everybody thinks this is such a great idea, why don't we do it? That is, why haven't we always interacted with our children in a way that reflects the qualities we want to teach, and why do we find ourselves falling so easily back in to the Cycle of Conflict? This is what the next chapter is designed to address.

Chapter 2

The Power of Our Past

Why is this "teaching by example" so rare and the Cycle of Conflict so common? Two words: our past. When I say "our past," I mean the experiences and/or role models that have taught us what a parent-child interaction should look like. By the way, this isn't about blaming our parents, it's just acknowledging that what we learned in our past may be having a powerful impact on how we react today.

The truth is that our past is where we first learned what it meant to be a parent, child, father, mother, sister, brother, husband, wife, etc. Our past was also where we learned what it meant to be powerful and powerless, or the person who *made* the rules versus the person or persons who had to follow those rules. Many of us became very clear, very fast that it was better to be the person making the rules than the person who had to "do what they were told." That's why, when you see a child interacting with a younger playmate or sibling, you will often see them playing the part of the parent or the "person in charge." Interestingly enough, they will often be using the same language and tone of voice that was used on them, which can at times be somewhat embarrassing for us as parents, when we happen to catch a glimpse of ourselves in our children's behavior. Remember, children don't always do what we say, they do what we do!

The Power of our Beliefs

The fact is, we learned many of our beliefs about what it means to be a parent by the way we were parented and how the culture in which we were raised in viewed the parent-child relationship. Further, these parental beliefs, paradigms, or mental models are likely to still be affecting our reactions in terms of how we interact with our children today. Now this isn't necessarily a bad thing. It's possible that many of the beliefs that we learned as a child can serve us very well today.

What I want to illustrate is how powerful these learned beliefs can be so that we can determine whether they are part of the problem or the solution. For you see, it's not always the facts, or what happens to us, that create our experience of life, but what we have learned to believe about ourselves and the world that determines how we are going to react to any given situation. The diagram below illustrates how our beliefs (paradigms, mental models, etc.) create our interpretations, or how we give meaning to what we see. These beliefs and interpretations then create our expectations (or what we expect to happen next) as well as how we feel, what we do, and ultimately, our entire experience of life.

This explains why different people can have very different reactions to the same situation. It's not the situation (or the facts) that is causing the reaction. It is how we interpret what we see, what we expect to happen next, and how we feel, which are all based upon our beliefs. Further, it doesn't stop there. Since our experience of life (how we feel and what we do) is created by what we believe to be true, we often find ourselves experiencing situations the same way again and again. This only goes to reinforce the "righteousness" of our original beliefs, which then goes on to influence what we feel and do next. All of this results in a self-fulfilling prophecy that is as powerful as the Cycle of Conflict we spoke of earlier.

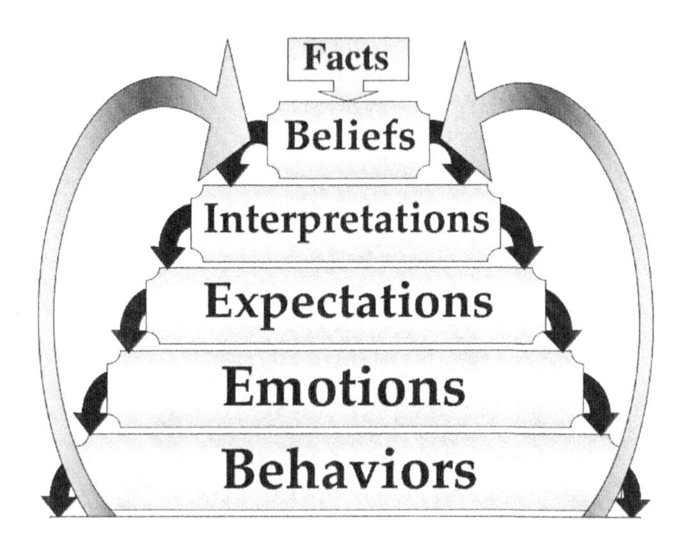

What does all of this have to do with parenting? Well, what did *you* learn about being a parent and raising kids? Do you agree with all of these learned perspectives? Do they all serve you well as a parent today? Do they help you inspire in your children the qualities that you want them to have as adults? Are they congruent with your highest purpose in terms of who you want to be as a parent?

The point here is that we all were influenced by the prevailing beliefs of our past, and those learned beliefs are having an impact on how we raise our children today. Unfortunately, those from whom we learned these beliefs may not have always been acting "on purpose" or in a way that was congruent with what *they* wanted to teach. That is, when we were being taught, corrected, or punished, our parents, teachers, or other authority figures may not have been thinking, *Here is an opportunity to reinforce qualities that I would like this child to have as an adult.* They were probably just trying to get us to do what *they* wanted based upon how *they* had been parented, or what they believed to be the "right way" to raise a child.

In fact, the model of parenting that was most prevalent when I grew up was that a good parent watched their children very carefully and pointed out what they did wrong so that they could correct the problematic behavior. Parents didn't say too much about what their children did well out of fear that their kids would get a "big head" or become conceited. I'm sure our parents thought that this would help us grow up to be happy, productive adults.

The problem with this philosophy, however, is that while we, as children, were learning who we were, and establishing our sense of self-worth, we were constantly being reminded of what we were doing wrong by those we loved and respected the most. This may have done more to teach us to become our "own worst critic" and fear making mistakes than support us in becoming happy, productive adults. It may also explain why so many people find themselves constantly fighting this nagging feeling that no matter what they do, it will never be good enough.

In any case, it's probably safe to say that we all have some habitual ways of interacting with our children that are incongruent with our highest purpose. The challenge is that if we are not aware of these habitual reactions, we will probably continue to repeat them. Therefore, the second step in the model (Our

Past) is about becoming aware of these tendencies so that we can avoid falling into old patterns of response. There is a great quote from Albert Einstein that speaks to the value of this raised awareness which says:

"Problems cannot be solved at the same level of awareness that created them."

This quote, in my opinion, also speaks to why we find ourselves caught in power struggles, or the Cycle of Conflict with our kids. We may be trying to solve the problem at the same level of awareness that created it. In other words, we might be "raising our kids" by watching for what they are doing wrong, and making it our job to correct them. And because our kids are egocentric (they hear us saying that *they* are bad versus what they are doing is bad), they resist hearing our correction and might even build up a resistance to hearing us in other areas.

What we might want to do, instead, is raise our awareness of what we want (versus what we don't want) and allow this new focus to guide our decisions about how we interact with our kids. In other words, the more we become aware of our highest purpose as parents (i.e. what we want our children to learn and who we want them to become), as well as, those response patterns that are incongruent with our purpose, the more influential we can become in their lives.

In order to ensure that you have become clear about which old response patterns or habits no longer serve you, now might be a good time to stop and write down some of the old thoughts or beliefs that have triggered these responses. The best way to identify these old beliefs is to compare your current habits (in terms of how you find yourself responding to your children) with the list of qualities you want your kids to have when they grow up. You will notice that some are congruent with this list while others are not.

For example, we may want our children to grow up to be good listeners who try to understand another's perspective as a way to resolve conflict. However, when there is a conflict between ourselves and our kids, we may not be listening and/or trying to understand *their* perspective, but instead just telling them how they are wrong and we are right! We may want them to grow up to be adults who learn from their mistakes and use this learning to come up with new and more creative ways of solving the problem. However, when they make a mistake, we may be trying to make them feel bad about what they did wrong, versus engaging them in a conversation about how they might do it differently next time.

While I believe that many of our old, habitual ways of thinking about parenting may not serve us, I also want to be clear that this isn't about blaming or bashing our parents. I'm sure that most of them loved us and were doing their best based upon what *they* experienced and were taught as a child. Instead, this is about becoming aware of the powerful influence our past (meaning our learned beliefs about parenting and children, etc.) can have on our experience of life today.

Further, I don't want you to get the idea that I believe everything we learned as a child was bad.

I'm sure that we all learned many valuable lessons about how to interact with children in a supportive and effective manner. In fact, I'm not here to pronounce anything as "good" or "bad." I just want to support you in being as clear as possible about what beliefs, learned perspectives, and ways of teaching you want to use with *your* children. That is, I want to support you in parenting and teaching "on purpose" so that you are interacting with your children in a manner that is both congruent with what you believe to be best for them now, and also teaches them the qualities that you want them to have as an adult. The question, of course, is how?

Chapter 3

The Wisdom of Serenity

If you remember in chapter one, as I began to discuss how to get kids to do what you want, I spoke of becoming clear about two things: (1) exactly what you do want, and (2) how you can get your children to cooperate with you versus becoming resistant and resentful. We have already addressed number one which is your highest purpose, and I *do* believe that the more purposeful we are in teaching positive qualities versus blind obedience, the more our children will cooperate with us versus resist us. I also believe that the work we did in chapter two (becoming aware of old beliefs that may be influencing your parental style in a way that doesn't serve you), will be an important step in helping you become as effective as possible.

However, as human beings in the roles of parents and teachers, we all know that there will be times when just being clear about what we want to teach won't be enough. There will be times when we are frustrated, exasperated, angry, tired, etc., and we will need more than a clear sense of purpose to help us deal with the situation effectively. This is what the rest of the book is about. The first two chapters were about the "what." What you want (your highest purpose) and what you don't want (your past, or old habits that are incongruent with this purpose). The next three steps, and the "real-life" application section that follows are designed to discuss the "how."

First, we must realize that it would be unrealistic to expect that we will never again find ourselves caught in the Cycle of Conflict or Resistance. Unfortunately, these are habitual reactions and, thus, we will probably find ourselves saying and doing things we know are incongruent with our purpose for some time to come. The question, therefore, becomes how do we break the cycle (before it breaks us), or how can we regain control of ourselves and the situation as soon as possible? The answer is simple, but not necessarily easy. As a matter of fact, this may be the most challenging part of the puzzle. I call it the "Wisdom of Serenity."

As some of you may know from reading my other books, my father was very active in the program of Alcoholics Anonymous, and my mother in Alanon. I grew up going to AA meetings and learning the value of changing one's life, and then helping others change theirs. Therefore, when I think of the "Wisdom of Serenity," I think first of the Serenity Prayer which, of course, says: *God grant me the serenity to accept the things I cannot change, the courage to change the things I can, and the Wisdom to know the difference.* What does this prayer have to do with getting children to do what we want? Well, for one thing, I believe that it describes the process by which it happens. Let me explain.

When we are stuck in a power struggle with our kids, trying to get them to do one thing or another while they seem to be focusing all of their will on resisting us, what do you think we need the most (other than a whip and a chair)? Well, given that our insistence is only creating more resistance, what I believe we need is serenity. We need to be able to stop, regain control of our thoughts and emotions and become more purposeful in our next response. We need to recognize that when the Cycle of Conflict is active, we are part of the problem versus the solution. In addition, trying to change our children so that we will feel less stressed isn't working. Therefore, we need to accept what we can't change (at least for the moment) and become aware of what we *can* change. Put another way, we need to focus on the aspect of the situation over which we have the most influence and control which, initially, is our response.

Now, don't get me wrong, I don't believe that we should just let our children do whatever they want and just become "serene" about it. Remember, my goal is to help you be *more* influential in the lives of your children. I just believe that, in order for us to become the influential, guiding force that our children need, we must first become clear about how we (our responses and behaviors) are affecting the situation. Then we can accept responsibility for that effect, and make responsible choices about what to do next. (Isn't that what we want our kids to do?)

Unfortunately for most of us, changing our response is the last thing we think of, and seemingly the hardest aspect of the situation to change. It seems so much easier to focus on the behavior of our children as the cause of our frustration, and attempt to change *them*. Sound familiar? How's that working for you?

Further, if our children do indeed learn by watching us (i.e. they have a tendency to "do what we do"), what are we really teaching them here? Aren't we in fact teaching them to blame those around them for their frustration rather than take personal responsibility for their emotions and behaviors?

Okay, what can we do instead? What if rather than focusing on changing them (which only seems to make them resist us even more) we, instead, create a moment of serenity, and focus first on what we can change (i.e. our response)? We can then begin to purposefully interact with our children in a way that is congruent with what we want to teach.

When I speak of "a moment of serenity," what I really mean is some way to stop "just reacting" and begin to choose our response. Kind of like when you were a child and you were angry or frustrated, and about to say or do something that you might later regret, one of your parents may have suggested that you first count to ten. This stopping and counting (or moment of serenity) gave you an opportunity to focus on something other than the problem and, thus, enhanced the likelihood that your next response, remark, or behavior would be more purposeful versus reactive.

Interestingly enough, the value of this old adage of counting to ten is now being confirmed by what we know of brain function. We actually have not one brain, but three, and each is a product of evolution. The oldest part of the brain is called the brain stem. We have this part in common with all reptiles (which is why it is called the reptilian brain) and this is where our fight-or-flight responses are primarily located. The next part of the brain to evolve was the limbic system and this is where many of our emotional responses reside. The third and most recent part of the brain to evolve is the neo-cortex which is the "thinking" part of our brain, meaning that this is where we make conscious choices about what to do next. If you look at the "reactions" side of the Cycle of Conflict or Resistance, you can see how many of these reactions are emotional and/or fight-or-flight in nature. Creating a moment of serenity allows us (or our neocortex, which is the purposeful part of our brain) to regain control and choose a response that is more purposeful or congruent with our highest purpose.

How you create this moment of serenity is, of course, up to you. Depending on the intensity of the situation, this could be as simple as a few deep breaths, walking away and regaining control, or actually leaving the scene for a longer period of time. Remember, one of our goals here is to teach our children how to deal with anger and/or frustration as well. How would you want your child to deal with *their* emotions as an adult?

In my fourth book, *Life from the Top of the Mind,* I spent the first part of the book describing a way to regain control when we find ourselves in the middle of a "stressful" situation. I call this the BRAIN model because it actually allows us to change the chemical make-up of our brain and body. If we were to apply this model to dealing with a stressful situation with our kids, it would mean that we would begin by seeing the stress or anxiety as a valuable signal that something isn't working. Rather than try to change our children, however (so that we would feel less stressed), we would begin to regain control by focusing on an aspect of the situation over which we have the most influence. We might begin by taking a few deep breaths and saying the word "relax" (or any word or phrase that to you represents serenity) on the exhale.

While breathing deeply won't solve the entire problem, it is a "neocortex" behavior, and thus allows us to influence the chemicals being produced by our brain and eventually change how we feel. Next, we might want to focus on the solution versus the problem by asking ourselves, "How would I rather be feeling, and if I were feeling this way, how would I be responding to my child?" or "How would I be responding to my child if I were responding "on purpose?" We could then use our imagination to create a mental picture of what this more purposeful response might look like, and what effect it might have on the situation. (For those of you who would like to understand this model more completely, please feel free to refer to my fourth book, *Life from the Top of the Mind.*

The good news is that as we breathe deeply, relax on the exhale, ask ourselves how we want to respond, and imagine responding that way, we will actually begin to change the chemical make-up of our brain and body and, thus, change how we feel. The bad news is that (even though one could go through this model in as little as ten to fifteen seconds), this may be too long a process for some. That's okay. Remember, this is about what works for you. For example, some of you might want to say a prayer, (the serenity prayer might be a good choice). Others might want to take a short walk or read a passage in a particular book. "How" you create this moment of serenity is less important than the degree to which this pause helps you refocus and begin to *practice* responding in a more purposeful manner.

I emphasize the word *practice* because I want to acknowledge that (a) it will take practice for us to become skillful at creating a moment of serenity in order to regain control of our response, and (b) this isn't about needing to be perfect as a parent and/or teacher. The truth is, of course, we are human beings, and as such, we will make mistakes. Despite our best efforts, there will be times when we will find ourselves reacting in ways we know are incongruent with our love for our children and our vision of how we want to be as their parent or teacher.

The good news, however, is that we can use these momentary lapses to teach yet another valuable lesson to our kids. We can show them how a person can make a mistake, learn from that mistake, and use this learning to make another choice. We might even let our kids in on what we are doing and why. In other words we might say something like: *"Hmmm, I notice that I am not responding to you in a way that I like. I'll tell you what, I'm going to go into the other room and calm down and think about how I want to help you learn from what just happened. Why don't you think about the situation as well, and we can talk later."*

Again, we are *always* teaching our children something, so why not use our own imperfections to teach them how to deal with *their* mistakes. How to stop (create a moment of serenity) and choose one's next response! Isn't this a quality that you would like your children to have as an adult?

So, congratulations! You're going to make mistakes! And now, even these miscues can become part of your teaching, and provide yet another valuable lesson for those who are observing you, and learning from your example.

Chapter 4

The Energy of Love Versus Fear

This discussion of mistakes leads us to another important consideration as we become skillful at getting our children to "do/be what we want." What I'm referring to is the *energy* we want to use (and of course, teach) as a guide for one's thoughts, decisions, and behaviors. The reason I mention this now, in conjunction with our discussion on mistakes, is that this topic provides a perfect illustration of how most of us were taught to use fear of bad things happening (such as worry about making or repeating mistakes) as a way to succeed in life. In fact, most of us were taught to worry about a lot of things, such as being abducted by strangers, doing poorly in school, not living up to our potential, etc.

"What's wrong with that?" you may be saying. "If being frightened of failure or harm helps keep our children safe and motivates them to succeed, what's the problem?" Well, let's return to your purpose, or the list of qualities that you want your child to have as an adult. Would it be accurate to say that "frightened" isn't on the list?

You see, if we teach our children through fear, then, in a sense, we are teaching them to trust fear (or to be frightened of failure, punishment, rejection, etc.) as a way to stay safe and succeed in life. And, even though this may be effective in the short term (i.e. having them do well on a test), the long-term ramifications are often less than satisfactory.

That's why "frightened" wasn't on your list of the qualities you want your children to reflect when they grow up. On some level you know that people who take or quit jobs out of fear, get into or out of relationships based on fear, or, in general, worry about all the bad things that can happen to them, are not happy, satisfied, productive adults, and certainly not the type of person you want your child to become. The type of individual you want your child to be is reflected in the list of qualities you made: trustworthy, honest, responsible, kind, compassionate, confident, etc. Do you see how the energy of "fear" is incongruent with these qualities?

There is another reason why choosing some energy other than fear as a foundation for teaching our children is important. As I mentioned earlier, when we are trying to get our kids to do what we want based upon fear, what we often do is try to make them feel bad about what they did, or are about to do, so that they will avoid that behavior in the future. In other words, we are encouraging them to worry about what they did or might do as a way to teach them not to do it. Can you see how and why this might not be the most successful teaching method? It has us and our children focusing on the problem versus the solution, and trying to use the pain of the problem as a motivation to change!

Further, when we worry about anything, what we are really doing is holding an image in our mind of what we ***don't want!*** It's like imagining (or worrying about) falling off a bicycle as a way to learn to ride. What we *may* learn is how to avoid getting hurt, however, the cost is that there is no energy or learning directed toward what we really want.

I'm going to guess that what you *really* want is for your children to learn to "do what's right" versus just avoid doing "what's wrong". If so, then we as parents/teachers must change our focus to the value of the solution, versus the fear of the problem.

What this means in real life is that when our children make mistakes (which, of course is guaranteed), our role is to help them focus on what they learned and what they might do differently the next time they find themselves in a similar situation (which is also guaranteed). This "solution-focused" approach also has the added benefit of not requiring that they feel bad about themselves (which they will resist) in order to learn the lesson. In fact, in addition to reducing their resistance to hearing our advice, this approach teaches several of the qualities that almost every parent wants their children to have, i.e., the ability to learn from their mistakes and have confidence in their choices and decisions.

Want an example? Let's look at the roles of actors and the director in making a movie. I use this illustration because these roles can be very similar to parents and children, except the participants are adults. For example, the director (much like a parent) has an idea or vision of how he/she would like the actor to play a scene. In other words, the director's role is to get the actors to do what he/she wants. The director knows that this process may require that the scene be shot (or taken) many times. Further, the director knows that if the actors lose confidence in themselves, they will become more likely to make mistakes, the quality of their work will go down, and the number of times the scene must be repeatedly shot will go up.

Therefore, when the actors make mistakes (which, of course is guaranteed), the director must respond in a way that both helps the actors learn *and* ensures that they will be motivated to apply this learning to future "takes". In a sense, a director must see a mistake as a "mis-take" or a take that missed, and focus on how the actors could do it differently next time. In this same way, we as parents can see our children's mis-takes as actions that they took (or takes) that missed. And, like a good director, we can help them learn from the mistake by focusing on the solution versus the problem, and give them the self-confidence to keep trying.

All of this is about using an energy other than fear as a motivator for your decisions and behavior with your children. What could this energy be?

Well, some call it "awareness", others, support, or optimism, I call it love. Love of learning by doing, trying, failing, and trying again. Love of who you are, who they are, and who you want them to become.

Another reason why I believe that we as parents and teachers should choose love versus fear as an energy for interacting with our children, is that it taps into our kid's natural desire to please their parents. I know, I know, sometimes it feels like this is the last thing on their little minds and yet, the truth is, on some level, ***our kids desperately want, and need our love and approval.***

If you doubt this, think back to when you were a kid. Do you remember how important and meaningful it was for you to receive praise from your parents? If you are like most of us, it was one of the most treasured experiences of life, and unfortunately for many, one of the rarest. Why was this experience so rare? Because many of our parents were following the philosophy that said the way to correct their kid's mistakes was by pointing out what they did wrong, and the way to teach them humility was playing down their successes.

I suggest that we as parents take a different approach, one that taps into our children's natural desire for love and approval. I further suggest that as we become skilled at harnessing this energy, we will have discovered one of the most powerful forces available for molding their lives. How can we do this***? By catching them doing something right!*** In the trainings I do with organizations, my colleagues and I call this process "stalking excellence". You can do this with your kids! Rather than always pointing out their mistakes, this new perspective has you attending to (and thus reinforcing) the positive, thoughtful, creative, loving, imaginative, joyful things that your children do every day. Point out how proud you are of them when they act this way. Let them know that you notice when they are displaying these admirable qualities (which are probably congruent with who you want them to be when they become adults).

Further, let them know that you see these positive traits as representative of their true nature, or who they really are. Let them know how these traits affect your desire to be around them and do things for, and with them. Give them as many reasons as possible to feel good about themselves and their choices so that they might choose this way of being again in the future.

This is what I mean by teaching through love versus fear, love of life, learning, others, themselves, you, nature, our planet, their friends, their school, their community, etc. versus fear of punishment, failure, shame, ridicule, making mistakes, and rejection. I believe that when we use this energy as a guide, we increase the likelihood that they will become the loving, responsible, trustworthy, compassionate, confident adults we want them to be.

Chapter 5

The Value of Responsibility

The last component in our "how to get kids to do what you want" model is the concept of *responsibility*. If you are like most parents and teachers, this is probably one of the items that you included on your list of the qualities that you want your children to reflect when they become adults. If not, I bet it's one that you would add in a heartbeat.

The concept of responsibility has at least two interpretations or definitions, both of which, I imagine, you would want for your child. The first definition is the most obvious. It means to take care of, or ownership of, and refers to one's ability to either take responsibility for one's possessions, or responsibility for performing one's duties. In the case of children, this would refer to their picking up their toys, clothes, taking responsibility for taking out the trash, etc.

The second definition is about being "responsible" or having the ability to respond.

Responsibility: One's ability to respond

This means that one has the ability to respond to any situation in a way that inspires trust, takes ownership, allows them to learn from both their successes and failures, and avoids blaming others for their reactions, emotions, etc.

How can we teach our kids to be responsible, or encourage them to take responsibility for their actions, feelings, words, possessions, etc.? Well, (as I'm sure you have noticed), I believe that the best way to teach our kids anything is to model the behavior or quality that we want them to learn *while we are teaching them the lesson!* So, how do we get our kids to be responsible? We begin by taking responsibility for ***our*** actions, words, emotions, possessions, duties, etc., especially when interacting with, and/or being observed by, our kids . . . and by letting them know that we are doing this "on purpose."

What this means in "real life" is that first we avoid blaming our kids (or anyone else) for our anger and frustration, or any behavior that results from these emotions. We avoid phrases like "You are making me so angry" or "If you don't want me to treat you like a baby, stop acting like one." Does this mean that we should never get angry at our kids? Of course not. Not only is this impossible, it would be teaching them that *they* should never get angry, and, thus, making them feel like failures when they do. Instead, what we can do is teach them how to handle or take responsibility for their anger and other emotions, while also addressing the problem at hand.

When we find ourselves getting angry at our kids (which is guaranteed), we might say something like: "I notice that I am very angry right now, and rather than getting in to an argument or saying something I might regret later, I'm going to take responsibility for cooling off, and thinking about how we can do this differently. Why don't you do the same and we can talk" (*then set a time to talk about the solution*).

You then come back at that appointed time (this is very important so that problems don't just get "swept under the rug") and discuss what you have learned, as well as, how you might apply this learning to a similar situation in the future (i.e. the solution). You can then ask your kids to do the same, or speak to what *they* have learned, and what *they* would do differently next time. I bet you will be amazed at how taking responsibility for your emotions and then focusing on a solution versus the problem (whose fault it was, or who is to blame) creates an atmosphere of problem-solving versus resistance. In addition, this process will very likely result in your kids being more motivated to hear what you have to say, and even participate in the learning process, versus defend themselves and their position. Further, a process such as this teaches them the value of having the ability to respond more purposefully to life versus being driven by our "righteous indignation" and/or old, habitual ways of reacting.

The question really becomes: Would we like our kids to be able to respond to life in a purposeful way? Would we like them to have the ability to notice how they are feeling, and then influence the quality of these emotions and behaviors without blaming others? If having this "ability to respond," is important, then we must model what it means to be responsible.

Further, I would encourage you to take 100% responsibility for your "ability to respond." This doesn't mean that we have to be perfect, in fact (as we have discussed), I think trying to be a perfect parent is a disservice to ourselves and our kids because it sets an impossible standard for everyone, and guarantees failure. Instead, taking 100% responsibility for the quality of our responses (and teaching this to our kids) just means that we are not going to blame our responses on them (or others), or wait for some person or situation to change before we respond to life in a purposeful manner.

Wouldn't it be great to have your kids come up to you and say "You know, Mom (or Dad), I've been thinking about what happened the other day when I was so upset, and I've got some ideas about what I might do differently if that happens again." If you are like most parents, this would be music to your ears. Well, have you ever said that to them? ***Remember,***

our kids don't always do what we say, they do what we do!

The bottom line is that the manner in which we interact with our kids, how we listen or don't listen, respect them or model disrespect, inspire them to cooperate or to resist and resent, take responsibility for how we feel and what we do, or blame others,... all of this teaches them how to interact with us, and everyone else in their life.

Therefore, the only question is, will the quality of our interactions with our kids and the lessons that are taught as a result be something our children will want to hang on to and use as a foundation for their success and happiness, or spend much of their life getting over? The good news is that, as parents and teachers, we are in the position to answer this question ***now***, in a very purposeful, powerful way, and our answer can be the greatest gift we could ever give to those we love who are looking to us for direction.

Chapter 6

Putting It All Together: The POWER of Parenting On Purpose

So, how can we bring all these concepts and ideas together in a way that gives us as parents (and/or teachers) some model or guide in becoming more influential with our kids? Well, let's look at the five-step model embedded in what we have discussed so far.

We begin with the concept of "parenting on purpose" and define our highest purpose with our kids as helping them acquire the qualities we want them to have as adults (your list). This list then becomes "what we want" and we look for opportunities to model/teach these qualities in our daily interactions with our children. The challenge with this first step (parenting on purpose) is to bring these qualities to life versus just remaining mere words on a page. The way to do this is to start with a vision of what they look like, or how we would be thinking, feeling, and interacting with our kids if we were doing it "on purpose".

For example, "honesty" is the result of doing or saying what? Responsibility is the result of what choices and actions? Confidence comes from what life experiences? If I were being honest, respectful, and responsible with my kids, what would this look like? How might this be different from the way I am interacting with them now (especially when I'm upset)?

The more we have a clear vision of what these qualities look like (and more specifically, what *we* would look like if we were using these qualities as guides) the higher the probability that we will be able to model these qualities with our kids. Therefore, I would encourage you to refer to your list often, and ask yourself each time you interact with your child (or at least each time you remember) *Which of these qualities do I want to teach now, and what would I be doing (i.e. what would my behavior look like, sound like, etc.) if I were teaching this concept?* I think you will be amazed at how this first step begins to lessen the conflict and resistance in your relationship with your children, and increases their motivation to cooperate with you.

The second step is to make sure you are aware of the old habits, beliefs, tendencies, and learned behavior that may be incongruent with your purpose. Remember Dr. Einstein's wisdom: "Problems cannot be solved at the same level of awareness that created them." This second step, therefore, is about raising your awareness so that you are actively choosing how you want to be with your kids versus just finding yourself reacting in ways that may be familiar (or familial) but not especially productive. As you practice raising your awareness, you may find these old ways of reacting are almost always present when your kids are being their most resistant. Good information!

It's not important to dwell on these old ways of being, or worry about the fact that we will find ourselves reacting this way despite our best efforts. We will. Because habits are habitual, there will be times when we will find ourselves thinking, saying, and / or doing things that we know are not congruent with our highest purpose, or what we want to teach. In fact, as you continue to practice "parenting on purpose," you will become more and more aware of when you are *not* following these guides, but instead reacting in some old, habitual way. Congratulations! Use this awareness to choose what you want to do next and let your kids know what you are doing. This way you will have not only begun a process that has you developing new, more purposeful habits, you will have taught your children a valuable lesson, as well... the lesson of using one's awareness to make choices about one's responses.

As I have mentioned earlier, these first two steps are important because they allow us to become clear about what we want and what we don't want (our purpose and the old habits that are incongruent with this purpose). The next three steps are about how to make the best use of this new awareness on a day-to-day basis.

The third step in the model is the "wisdom of serenity" and involves our ability to stop, refocus, become clear about what we want and don't want, and then proceed in a way that is congruent with our highest purpose. It also allows us to avoid falling into the trap of trying to change our kids first (which they interpret as being told that they are not good enough and, will, therefore, understandably resist). Instead, we become skilled at (a) creating a moment of serenity, (b) accepting what we can't change (we don't try to deal with our stress by first changing our kids), (c) accepting them for who they are (human beings who may be making a mis-take), and, (d) changing what we can, which is initially our response. As a result, we may be surprised at how this actually reduces our kid's resistance to our authority and (ironically) motivates them to be more willing to cooperate with us, or do what we want.

Further, when we are willing to practice serenity on a daily basis versus waiting for the crisis to happen, we can bring this more consistently calm perspective to *all* aspects of our lives, and, thus, become that much more prepared when the not-so-occasional crisis *does* come our way. Plus, we will be teaching our kids the value of serenity as a precursor to accepting what they can't change and having the courage to change what they can. Not a bad lesson, don't you think?

Next, if we have determined that the energy of love, awareness, confidence, etc. is more congruent with the qualities that we want to teach than fear, we can become skilled at using these energies as a guide in dealing with our kids. Now, the challenge here is that many of us have learned that one of the ways parents demonstrate their love for their children is to worry about them. We have confused caring with worrying. You may have even heard a parent (or yourself) say "Hey, if I didn't care about you, I wouldn't worry!"

Now granted, there are parents out there who seem not to care for their kids and, therefore, seem never to be concerned about where they are and what they are doing. And if you are choosing between worrying about your kids or not caring, I would encourage you to choose worrying. I believe, however, that there is a third choice that is more congruent with what you really want. In other words, unless "worry" and "fear" are the qualities you want to teach, I would encourage you to avoid jumping to the conclusion that "good parents worry". What we are really talking about here is caring, awareness, and love. Good parents care enough to be aware of what is going on in the lives of their children. While I can understand how many of us may have grown up watching our parents take this desired awareness and express it as worry, I'm going to suggest that you make a more purposeful choice.

For example, let's imagine Johnny comes home and asks if he can go and play with the new kid that just moved in down the street. If we as parents were using fear and worry to keep our children safe, we might say something like: *"Oh I don't think so. We don't know who these people are. They may have loaded guns in their house. You know, you just can't go around trusting everyone you meet. Why don't you just find something to play with in your room where I know you will be safe?"*

What would we be teaching here? What do you think Johnny would learn about connecting with others or even the world, in general?

So, what should we do, just start singing "Don't worry, be happy" and let him go play in an unfamiliar situation? No! *Remember, we are not choosing between worrying and caring.* We are choosing to respond from an energy that is congruent with our highest purpose (or the qualities that we want our children to have as adults) and unless worry and fear are among those qualities, using fear of bad things happening to keep our children safe would be incongruent with this higher purpose.

So, what's our alternative? Well, if we wanted to teach how to make good decisions using awareness and love, we might say something like: *"How nice of our new neighbors to invite you over. You know, I've been meaning to go and welcome them to the neighborhood and just haven't made the time. I tell you what, if you can give me a minute, I will go with you and meet your new friend and his parents, and we can see if they share our beliefs about safety and kids. If so, then you can play over there for a while, If not, then you can invite your new friend over here to play. Okay?"*

Now, again, you might have said this differently, plus this conversation assumes that you have already talked to your child about what a "kid-safe" home looks like. As always, the point of these examples isn't to tell you how you should parent your child. The point is to demonstrate the difference between using fear versus awareness as guides to making decisions about your children's safety, and, thus, teaching them about how to make their own decisions in the future.

The final step in understanding how the concepts we have discussed combine to create a powerful philosophy of "parenting on purpose"is our willingness to take 100% responsibility for our actions, reactions, emotions, home, possessions, etc., and, thus, teach this concept of responsibility to our kids. The key here is to identify whether "the ability to respond" to life in a purposeful way is an important quality you want your children to have, and if so, look for opportunities to teach this ability or quality.

Unfortunately, most children learn what has been referred to as "the blame game" where, when confronted with a problem, the goal seems to abdicate one's own responsibility and find someone to blame. This is evidenced by the familiar playground cries of "Well, she started it" or "He hit me first" or "Mommy, Johnny's teasing me"... "I am not!" "Are too!" etc. This need to find fault is based upon the belief that the solution lies in finding the person "responsible" for the problem, and from this perspective comes the concept of "responsibility equals blame." It's no wonder, therefore, kids seem to balk at the lesson of "responsibility." Most are afraid that it means if something goes wrong and I'm responsible, "it's my fault."

If, however, you are wanting your child to become more responsible, following this "responsibility = blame" line of thinking probably isn't working for you. How do you change? You first change the meaning of the word in terms of how you interact with your children. One good way to begin this process is to look for examples of your children's success and begin to pair the concept of responsibility with what they are doing well. Comments like "Wow, are you responsible for this great drawing?" can have your children answering "Yes" to the concept of being responsible.

Next, you can verbally acknowledge when you are taking responsibility for *your* possessions and/or chores by saying things like: "Looks like I need to take responsibility for cleaning up this mess I made", or "picking up my dirty clothes," or "doing my chores," etc.

You can also begin to tap into your children's internal motivation to take more responsibility by rewarding responsible behavior. Again, the best time to do this is after they have done something well. You might say something like *"Wow, Johnny you have done a great job of taking responsibility for putting your bike away. I'm very proud of you!"* The goal here is to make "being responsible" a positive experience, one that your child would want to repeat, versus a criticism, or correction.

Finally, as we discussed in the previous chapter, we can begin to broaden the meaning of the word responsibility to include one's "ability to respond" by speaking to **our** ability to respond, especially when we lose it. Since one of the times we would like our children to be able to apply this "ability to respond" is when they are reacting inappropriately, the best way to teach this quality is to verbalize how we might use this skill (being able to choose our response) under similar circumstances.

For example, after losing our temper we might

say something like, *"Hmmm, you know what? I'm not happy with the way I just responded to (fill in the blank with what just happened). I think I am going to rethink this situation, and choose another response."* Granted, this is not an easy thing to do, but what a gift we will be giving to our children if we can demonstrate how someone can take responsibility in life versus seeing oneself as a failure, or looking for someone to blame.

In addition, we can look for opportunities to give *them* the ability to respond or make choices for themselves as much as possible. While it is often true that we will know "what's best for our kids" we must be willing to give them the opportunity to make choices, and learn from these choices as they mature. It is unreasonable to believe that children who grow up having their decisions made for them will miraculously one day become adults who can make decisions for themselves.

Now, of course, the choices we allow them to make will depend upon their age and maturity. You naturally wouldn't give a five-year old the same freedom of choice that you would a child of eleven. However, it has been my observation that we, as parents, tend to error on the side of fewer choices, regardless of the age. Our challenge is to keep in mind that we want them (and even expect them) to be making responsible, adult choices by say, age eighteen, nineteen, or twenty, (at the latest) and, therefore, should be giving them the opportunity to learn how to make choices from a very early age.

Of course, there will be choices that we will make for them when they are very young. Most of these revolve around their safety, nutrition, etc. These are healthy boundaries, because we know that if the child were to go beyond these, they would be in danger.

Below is a visual representation of the boundaries we set for our children, and how those boundaries should change if we are wanting to support them in becoming confident adults.

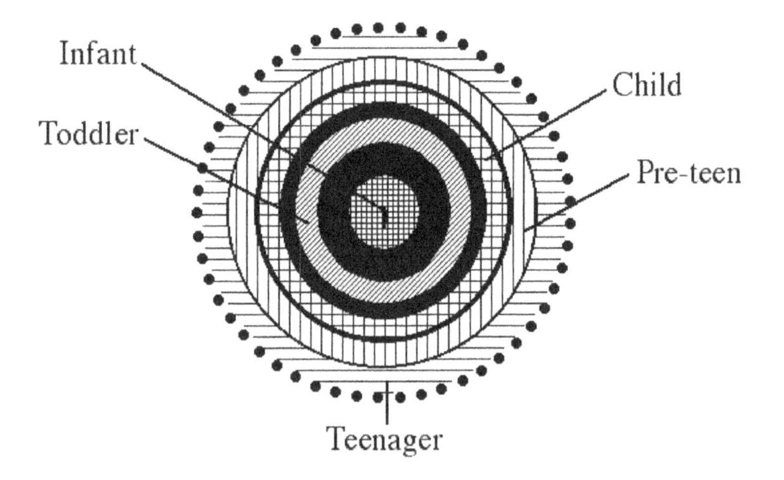

As you can see, the boundaries are very firm and clear when they are young, and become more flexible and transparent as they age and mature so that when they are finally "on their own," they have become skilled at making quality decisions. This graphic can also reflect the aspect of parenting that is often the hardest, the fact that from the moment we hold them close as babies, the rest of our life will be a process of "letting go". The challenge for us as parents seems to be to not only ensure that these boundaries change (and even fade) as our children grow, but to also look for opportunities for our children to make choices for themselves within those boundaries as they mature.

Choices such as what clothes to wear, how they spend their time, etc. can be wonderful learning opportunities for our children to practice making decisions. The good news is that even if they make the wrong choice, they can learn from the experience much more effectively than if we had told them what to do.

So, how can we insure that our children grow up to be the responsible, loving, confident, purposeful adults we want them to be? As the title of this chapter suggests, we first look for opportunities to respond to, or teach our children "on purpose," knowing that our interactions with them are the most powerful form of influence we have. As we model the qualities we want them to have as adults, being aware of our past habits, using the wisdom of serenity to stop and "re-center" every so often, choosing to teach from love versus fear, and taking 100% responsibility for *our* ability to respond, we give them an excellent model of the sort of adults we want them to be.

Purpose
Our Past
Wisdom of Serenity
Energy of love vs. fear
Responsibility

In this case, the purpose of the model is to help us as parents become more powerful and influential in the lives of our children, while, at the same time, allowing our kids to become more powerful or influential in their own lives. In addition, given that we are teaching qualities such as respect, honesty, responsibility, and compassion by interacting with our children in respectful, honest, responsible, and compassionate ways, we are less likely to find ourselves creating power struggles with our kids. This means that our children will be less likely to fear "losing" with us and, thus, be less resistant and more cooperative.

Put another way, "parenting on purpose," or becoming a "solution-focused parent" means that we are willing to interact with our children in ways that model the qualities that we want them to have as adults. This not only teaches them the things we most want them to learn, it creates a relationship that has them more open to following our direction, or... (surprise!) . . . "doing what we want".

Chapter 7

Breaking The Power Struggle

Remember the Cycle of Conflict? I introduced this in the first chapter to illustrate how our response to our children being "difficult" could create a cycle that has a tendency to grow increasingly destructive, often resulting in everyone feeling discouraged, angry, and resentful.

Certainly the concepts we have discussed up to this point can play a powerful role in diffusing this cycle, however, they are just concepts and, therefore, they can be difficult to translate into specific behaviors. What I would like to do in this second half is discuss specific ways of breaking the power struggle, or diffusing the Cycle of Conflict.

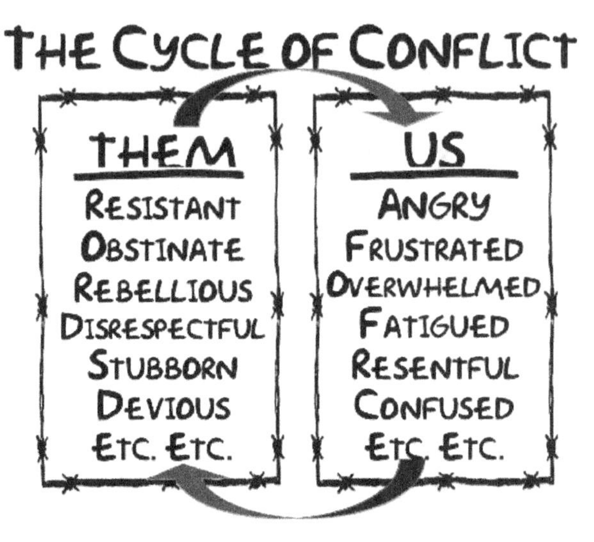

If you remember, one of the premises of this book is the quote from Albert Einstein that says "Problems cannot be solved at the same level of awareness that created them". Therefore, in order to keep our problematic interactions with our kids from turning into a cyclic power struggle, we must raise our awareness of what is driving this cycle from both our perspective, and the perspective of our children.

For example, chances are that if anyone came upon us after we had just experienced a problem with our child and asked us why we were so upset, we would have no problem telling them. *"Well, they were being (this way or that way) and I tried to reason with them, but they just (fill in the blank with whatever response we didn't like.)"* In other words, we know why *we* are upset at them, but do we *really* understand why they are being so resistant? In fact, isn't it common to hear parents say *"I don't understand why Johnny gets so upset when I tell him something. I'm just trying to (fill in the blank with something that is "for his own good".)*

Bottom line, if we really want to be influential with our kids we must also raise our awareness/understanding of what's going on with them. Given that in addition to teaching them the qualities we want them to have as adults, our purpose is to get them to hear and value our advice and direction, let's raise our awareness of the barriers that might be keeping this from happening. In other words, let's look at what might be driving their "difficult behavior," and what we can do to minimize their resistance and maximize their potential to hear our suggestions and ideas as valuable.

Listening Versus Talking

One of the barriers that can interfere with our children listening to us is their need for us to listen to them. In other words, often they have something that they want or need to tell us, and they are afraid that we won't listen, which can result in their becoming more frustrated and resistant. This isn't hard to understand if we recall (even as an adult), the times that *we* had something that we wanted to tell someone, but they weren't listening. Do you remember how frustrating that experience was, and how we tended to become more and more "difficult," trying to get the other person to listen? This is often even more frustrating for a child because, as a rule, children aren't listened to by adults. Take your own childhood, for example, especially when there was a problem or conflict. Did your parents, as a rule, sit down and really listen to your side of the story? If you are like most of us, the answer is "no". Now remember, this isn't about blaming our parents, it's just about recognizing that most of us grew up being told to listen versus being listened to. Therefore, we learned that those in power did the talking, and the less powerful (in this case, children) were supposed to listen.

Do you remember how frustrating that was, being forced to listen to someone when you had something you really wanted, even needed them to hear? It was so frustrating that we probably weren't really listening to the adult, and certainly weren't hearing the adult's admonitions as valuable information.

Now remember, this discussion isn't about whether or not children should listen to their parents. Of course they "should" and yet, often, they don't. Our purpose here is to diffuse the Cycle of Conflict, and remove the obstacles to our children hearing our advice and guidance as the valuable information that it is. I'm suggesting that one of these obstacles is our tendency to be talking to them (or taking the "active role" in a conversation by telling them what we want them to know) when they have something they need to tell us. When this is happening, the likelihood that our children will hear what we are saying as valuable is not very high.

Remember also, the premise of this book is that our interactions with our children influence how *they* learn to interact with the world. Therefore, if one of the qualities that we want them to have as adults is the ability to listen to others (especially when there is a conflict), then the best way to teach them is to model this quality. This is called taking a "receptive position," and I am going to suggest that (a) this is a more powerful position (than the active role) when dealing with conflict, and (b) the best way to help them learn that quality is by modeling it, or listening to them.

Further, in addition to modeling / teaching what we want them to learn, and lessening their frustration (of needing to say something but not being heard), our willingness to take a receptive position and listen to them has other benefits, as well. For example, when someone is needing to tell you something, chances are that at least to them, this "something" is very important. Therefore, when we are willing to hear what our children need to tell us, not only are we removing one of the barriers to their listening to us, we are learning what is important to them. If our goal is to tap into their internal motivation to listen, knowing what is important to them should be important to us! Therefore, it would serve us to not only listen to what is important to them, but stop every so often and check to see if we are hearing them accurately. I realize that this sounds like a lot of trouble, however the alternatives are (a) not listening to them at all, (b) pretending to listen to them, but really just waiting until they run out of steam, and (c) listening, and then assuming that we are understanding them correctly. I am going to suggest that none of these alternatives truly serve us or our children.

For example, have you ever had someone just "pretend" to listen to you? Have you ever had someone assume they knew what you were trying to say, but they were wrong? If so, you know how any of these responses can stifle communication, and given that communication is our goal here, I am going to suggest that listening to our children and even stopping every so often to check to see if we are "getting it right" is worth the effort. Wouldn't you want them to do this with you?

Often, another barrier to our children hearing what we have to say is their fear that we don't understand them, or the seriousness of their problem. For teenagers, this mantra of *"You just don't understand"* often seems to be all they say. Of course, we think we *do* understand and, yet, have you noticed that when we respond to our children with *"Yes, I do!"* they don't seem too thrilled? In fact, they seem to just get more upset, and begin to defend the seriousness of their problem, and their right to be upset.

If we truly don't want them defending either of these perspectives (the seriousness of their problem, or their right to be upset) then we need to empathize with them in a way that conveys that we *can* understand how whatever problem they are having or whatever they are wanting us to know is important to them and could make them upset.

This can be as simple as saying (after we have first listened to them, of course) something like *"You know, I can see how important this is to you"* or *"I can see how you would be upset by this."* This doesn't, by the way, necessarily mean that we agree with them, or even that *we* would be upset under similar circumstances. It just allows us, by seeing the situation from their perspective, to move past their fear that we don't understand, so that we can begin to move toward an effective solution.

Agreement Versus Understanding

Here, it is very important not to confuse agreement with understanding. While we won't always *agree* with our children, we *can* work to understand how (from their perspective) they might be upset. As a matter of fact, if we *can't* understand why their problem would be important or upsetting to them, we have confirmed their fears about being misunderstood, and essentially blocked their eventual willingness to trust us, or listen to our solution. After all, in their mind, if we can't understand how they would be upset, we must not truly understand the problem. And if we don't understand the problem, how could we offer a workable solution? Further, if they feel that we are labeling them as "over-reacting," they are likely to turn their efforts to defending the rightiousness of their being upset and the seriousness of their problem. This, of course, is a position that we don't want them defending, and certainly one that is incongruent with our purpose of effective communication and problem-solving.

So, we begin by listening to them, checking to make sure that we are hearing them correctly, and then empathizing with them so they no longer feel misunderstood and / or the need to defend their emotions or position. Do we then begin to tell them our ideas, or what we want them to know? Well, we could, because chances are they are now more willing to hear and understand us because we have demonstrated that we understand what is important to them. However, I am going to suggest that we take one more step before we begin telling them what we want them to know.

The reason I am suggesting this extra step is that, as I have said earlier, the more we can interact with our children in ways that are congruent with the qualities we want them to have as adults, the better for all concerned. So then the question becomes, do you want your children to have the ability to come up with their own solutions to the problems and challenges they will face? If so, before you give them your solutions, ask for theirs!

This can be as simple as asking: *"Do you have any ideas about how to solve this problem?"* or if we are trying to help them learn from their mistakes, we could ask: *"Knowing what you know now, how would you do this differently in the future?"* You see, along with the fear that we don't listen and that we can't understand where they are coming from, most children (especially adolescents) believe that we, as parents, don't value their thoughts and ideas. Therefore, they may be thinking *"Hey, if you don't care about my ideas, why should I care about yours?"*

Again, we *want* them to care about, or value our input, and so we need to teach this by caring enough to ask about *their* ideas and solutions. Plus, they may have some really good ideas! Yes, believe it or not, sometimes our children might come up with solutions that are as good as, or even better than ours. If this happens, all the better, because they are much more likely to support solutions that they created. Plus, we are reinforcing the concept that they are intelligent individuals who can create successful solutions. Isn't this one of the qualities that you want them to have as adults?

Here I want to make one important point.

Up until now, we have been discussing the receptive skills of listening, empathizing (understanding) and asking for their solutions. In addition to dealing with many of the barriers to our children being willing to listen to us, these receptive skills also have the effect of absorbing their resistance and then allowing us to (lovingly) move the conversation toward a solution. I say "lovingly" because if we use these skills to try to trick or manipulate our kids, it won't work.

I'm not saying that our attempts at manipulation will not have any effect. I'm just saying that they won't motivate our kids to do what we want. What our attempts to manipulate our children *will* do, however, is teach them that the way to deal with conflict is to pretend to be interested in another's perspective so that you can manipulate them into going for yours. Sooner or later this tactic will fail, and our kids will become known as manipulators whom no one can trust. My guess is that this isn't one of the qualities that you want them to have as adults.

Now, I am not saying that we should always just be "receptive" with our kids. There will be times (especially when they are young) when being active versus receptive will be in their best interest. I *am* saying, however, that if we are never, or even rarely "receptive" in our interactions with our children, they are not likely to be receptive to us, or become skilled at being receptive to others.

Another of the barriers or factors in our children's resistance is their fear that if we win, they lose. This isn't hard to understand given how often what we want seems to be directly opposite to what they want, and of course, as parents, we have more power than they do, which means, more times than not, we win.

However, given that "losers" isn't how we want them to see themselves as adults, our challenge is to interact with them in a way that not only taps into their motivation to cooperate, but does so in a way that has them feeling like they are part of the solution.

This is the value of learning the difference between approaching an interaction from an active or receptive stance. If we are willing to begin by being receptive (especially when we notice that our kids are being actively resistant), we can deal with their barriers to communication, which are their fears that we don't care enough to listen, understand, and ask them about their ideas. Then, if we still believe that we have something to add, we can begin to frame our ideas or solutions in a way that incorporates what's important to them. Again, this makes it more likely that our children will be open to hearing what we have to say, and willing to try our solutions.

Here we might say something like: *"Having listened to what you've been saying, I've got some ideas about how to solve this if you're interested."* It's in the framing of our solutions or ideas that we begin to take a more active role, and we do this in a manner that respects and even incorporates their ideas into a solution that we all can support.

As we practice framing the solution in this more respectful manner, there are several ideas that will increase the potential for success. First, we need to be sure that this is the right time to offer a solution. The right conversation at the wrong time is the wrong conversation. As we have discussed earlier, often just postponing the discussion by a few hours or even a day can give all parties involved time to cool down and rethink the situation.

Second, there is one word that can make a huge difference in our kid's willingness to listen to us. You see, while many people have learned to acknowledge another's position before offering their own, they often use words that undermine the potential for success. For example, they might say something like: *"Okay, I see what you are saying, BUT . . . ."* The word "BUT" is the problem because it has a tendency to negate anything that comes before it. It's like beginning a conversation with a member of your family by saying, *"I really love you, BUT. . . . "* Chances are they are not going to be too open to hearing what comes next.

Changing that one word from "BUT" to "AND," however, can make a huge difference in how our ideas are received. For example, we might say *"I see what you are saying AND I've got some ideas about this, as well."* While this change doesn't guarantee that our ideas will be accepted, it does go a long way toward reducing our children's resistance because it doesn't negate their perspective. It just adds information to the discussion. Further, it increases the chances that everyone involved will create "both/and" versus "either/or" solutions. "Both/and" solutions draw from the perspective of all concerned and create the possibility of a win/win outcome versus the win/lose option that has either us or our children feeling frustrated, resentful, and/or defeated.

The best way to begin this more "active" role is to look for common ground, or things that both you and your children want. Their independence is often one of these common goals, as is your desire for them to become more skilled at making good decisions. Often, when our ideas are framed with these types of common goals in mind, the discussion is less likely to digress into one about "who's right" or "who wins."

So, how can we get our kids to do what we want and / or minimize their resistance while teaching them the communication skills we want them to have as adults? We can listen to them, empathize with them, ask them for their ideas, and then problem-solve by blending what's important to them with what's important to us. Make sense? Yet, if you have ever tried to communicate with your child in this manner, you know how difficult it is. Why? Well, consider this. When you were a child and there was a conflict in your home, how many of you had parents who modeled the conflict resolution skills of listening, empathizing, and asking you about your ideas before they offered their solutions? If you are like 99.9% of us, this just didn't happen.

Now, remember, this isn't about blaming our parents, it's about understanding why we find this model of communication so difficult. For the vast majority of us it is totally unfamiliar! Therefore, even if you have found this discussion valuable, it may take somewhat of a leap of faith for you to be able to implement this more purposeful model of parenting. That's why I call the model we have been discussing the LEAP model (<u>L</u>isten, <u>E</u>mpathize, <u>A</u>sk and <u>P</u>roblem-solve).

Listen
Empathize
Ask Them
Problem Solve

Because most of us didn't grow up in homes where this behavior was the norm, we must have faith that this more purposeful way of creating relationships with our kids will indeed help teach them the qualities that we want them to have as adults. Further, we must be willing to practice this way of being, or take the LEAP of faith necessary to become skilled at this new way of communicating.

Up to this point, we have not only outlined a model for interacting with our children "on purpose" (The POWER Model), we have described many of the barriers that could interfere with this more purposeful style of communication, and identified another model for dealing with these barriers (L.E.A..P). There is, however, one more barrier that deserves our attention, and this may be the biggest obstacle to getting our kids to listen and cooperate. The barrier I am referring to is our children's fear that we are going to blame or criticize them. In fact, I am going to suggest that whenever children are afraid that they are going to be blamed or criticized, they tend to stop listening to whatever is being said.

Now, I'm not saying that parents should never blame or criticize their children. Once again, I'm just wanting to help you as a parent become more influential in the lives of your kids by raising your awareness of what might be interfering with your being heard. I think it 's easy to see how a child who believes that he or she is being blamed or criticized would tend to resist hearing, or acting upon whatever is being said. And yet, if we as parents were to become aware of the percentage of time that we find ourselves interacting with our children in this critical way, we would probably find the number disturbingly high.

The good news is that I have a relatively simple way to avoid falling into this negative, critical trap. I call it the "You Stupid Idiot Rule". Quite simply, the "You Stupid Idiot Rule" says that we, as parents, should never say anything to our children in a way that we (or they) could end our statement with, "You stupid idiot". For example, *"Johnny! You've done it again! How many times have I told you not to do that? (you stupid idiot)"* or *"No, Sally, you can't go to that party! Why do you keep asking when I have already told you no! (you stupid idiot)"* Now, I know that upon reading this, many of us might be thinking: *"Oh no, now I won't be able to talk for the next three months"...* Remember, I said it was simple, not necessarily easy.

Unfortunately, even though we love our children and would never want them to think of themselves as stupid idiots, for many of us, this form of critical interaction is all too familiar. We become frustrated and angry, and our tone of voice has "You stupid idiot" written all over it. Plus, this has become a habitual pattern of communication that we may be repeating without even being aware that we are doing so.

The problem, of course, is that not only do our children resist following our direction when they feel blamed and / or criticized, they can begin to see themselves as we are unconsciously characterizing them. Remember, children, especially when they are young, tend to find their identity in their parent's eyes. In other words, they define themselves partly by how we interact with them. This is apparent in families where children are defined as "the slow one,""the pretty one," "the rebellious one," etc. Often, these become self-fulfilling prophecies that can affect their choices and perceptions of themselves for years to come.

If, indeed, our purpose is to instill in our children the qualities we want them to have as adults, as well as, to tap into their motivation to cooperate, then we must raise our awareness of how we are speaking to them. The "You Stupid Idiot" rule is about recognizing that if, as a result of interacting with us, they feel blamed, criticized, or diminished, our purpose is not being served. Therefore, the last step in the model is about speaking to our kids in a way that doesn't put them on the defensive (or remembering the "You Stupid Idiot" rule) which turns the LEAP model in to the LEAPS model.

Listen
Empathize
Ask Them
Problem Solve
Speak in a way that doesn't put them on the defensive.
(The "You Stupid Idiot" Rule)

This makes the LEAP model plural, which is appropriate in that it will likely take many "leaps of faith" for us to become skilled at this new, more purposeful way of interacting with our kids. The result, however, is that we will model the qualities of listening, understanding, and engaging another in creating successful solutions. And possibly most important, we will be doing this in a manner that shows consideration and respect (two qualities that I'm sure you would want your children to learn from you.)

If you remember, we started this discussion by talking about the value and power of the receptive position when our children are being resistant. We have also discussed that the reason we find this receptive stance so difficult is that most of us grew up with the powerful people in our lives taking the *active* role and expecting us to be receptive, or to listen, understand, and obey them. In fact, many of us grew up being told that our willingness to obey our parents, even if we disagreed with them, was a measure of our love and respect for them.

Is it any wonder, therefore, that we find ourselves taking this same active role with *our* children and expecting *them* to be obedient? And further, that we may find ourselves measuring how much *they* love and respect *us* by the degree to which they obey us without protest? In fact, we may even measure our success as parents by this yardstick, meaning that we see ourselves as good parents when we produce obedient children.

"What's wrong with obedient children" some may ask? Nothing if we are wanting to raise them to be "obedient" adults. However if instead, we are wanting them to grow up to be confident, independent, compassionate decision-makers, then we might want to help them see themselves in this way from the beginning.

A helpful analogy here might be to look at the difference between training puppies and raising kids (or adults). When we are training puppies, we are teaching them obedience because that's what we want them to grow up to be... obedient, adult dogs! We train them to respond to our commands and may even use punishment combined with other forms of teaching to ensure that they become well-trained, obedient pets.

With children, however, our purpose is very different. Most of us would say that our goal as parents is to teach our kids to become intelligent, self-sufficient, independent, caring adults, who have confidence in their ability to make their own decisions and succeed in life. And yet, I'm sure we all have seen homes where the parents seem to speak to both their children and their pets in the same tone of voice, sometimes even using the same commands.

Please keep in mind that I am not saying that children shouldn't obey their parents, or that the communication between a parent and a child should be some form of egalitarian democracy. I am just pointing out that how we interact with our kids may be a product of what we have learned rather than what we have chosen as most effective, so that we as parents can ask ourselves some important questions. Such as: *Is this working for us?* Meaning (a) is our tendency to take the active role and expecting our kids to listen and obey teaching them the qualities we want them to have as adults? (b) Is this method of parenting resulting in our children hearing our advice and direction as valuable information? (c) Is this teaching them to interact with others (maybe even *their* children) by talking or listening, understanding or demanding, working toward a solution that represents the ideas of everyone, or trying to convince others of the superiority of their way of thinking?

Bottom line . . . the question we need to ask ourselves as parents is: Are we interacting with our children "on purpose," or are we just reacting from some learned perspective that is more about obedience than modeling the qualities that we want them to have as an adult? And of course, the most important question: "How is this working for us and our children?"

Chapter 8

Choices, Agreements, Rewards, & Encouragement

Before we move into a discussion about how to apply all of this in "real life", I want to introduce one final model with the goal of giving you as many tools as possible to support you in becoming more influential in the lives of your kids. This model has four components and fits very well with both the POWER model and the LEAP model. The four components are *choices, agreements, rewards,* and *encouragement.*

Choices

We have talked a lot about choices, but I'm not

sure that we have discussed the reason this is such an important component in succeeding with your children. To understand why this is so important, we must understand the experience of being a child. Much of a child's life is decided and directed by others. Well-meaning others, to be sure. However, let's acknowledge the possibility that when our children are being resistant, they may be feeling powerless, as if they have no choice in what happens to them. And this powerless perspective is incongruent with who we want them to become as adults.

Of course, sometimes they will *not* have a choice because they are not old and/or mature enough to make whatever decision is at hand and that is just part of being a child. While this is very understandable from our point of view, it can be very frustrating to our children, and this frustration can contribute to their resistance. Given that one of our goals is to reduce their resistance, one way we can do this is to give them as many choices as possible.

The challenge, of course, is to give them choices in such a way that everyone wins. In other words, *they* feel as if they have some influence in their lives (and that they become skilled at making good choices), and we get them to do what we want them to do, and/or become who we want them to be. The way to do this is to make sure that we frame or present the choices we give them so that we are okay with whatever they choose. For example, let's assume that Jenny is watching TV or listening to music at a volume that is disturbing others. Some parents might say: *"Jenny! Turn that down! I can't even hear myself think!"*

While this *might* achieve our goal of having Jenny turn down the TV, it's not likely to help her grow up to be a considerate person because (a) the parents are not modeling consideration in the way they interacted with her, and (b) she is likely to feel resentment toward her parents for talking to her in what she is likely to hear as a demeaning tone of voice. In fact, one could have easily put *"You stupid idiot!"* on the end of the command. The bottom line was that "how" the problem was addressed was very likely incongruent with Jenny's parents highest purpose, to teach Jenny the qualities that they want her to have as an adult.

How could we approach this in a more purposeful and a more successful manner? Well, we might say something like: *"Jenny, I'm sure you don't mean to disturb others, and yet the volume of your (TV/boom box/whatever) is kind of loud. Would you rather turn it down, or turn it off and do something else?"* Here we have done several things. We have reinforced that she isn't the sort of person who would knowingly disturb others (a positive adult quality) *and* given her the opportunity to choose how she handles the solution. Now, I'm not saying that this will necessarily motivate Jenny to respond with *"Thank you, Mom/Dad for your allowing me the freedom to choose".* In fact, she may even just give us a frumpy look and turn it down. However, what is important is that she will have made the choice, and we interacted with her in a way that modeled consideration and respect, qualities that we would want her to have as an adult.

We will have more examples of the value of choices in the scenarios to follow. Until then, just remember that when people (and especially children) feel that they have some choice in the situation, they are less likely to resist our influence and/or defend their position. In other words, they are more likely to do do what we want.

Agreements

The second component in this final model revolves around making *agreements.* As with the concept of choices, we have discussed agreements earlier, however, I believe that this concept is so important it deserves special attention because agreements are what allow us to shift our focus from teaching "obedience" to the qualities we want our children to have as adults. In fact, I would suggest that the ability to make and keep agreements is one of the most critical components of becoming a successful adult.

So, how can we teach our children the skill of making and keeping agreements? Well, of course, we must first make sure that we are modeling this skill by making clear agreements with our kids, and then keeping them! This may sound easy, however, if you are like most parents, you know that there have been, and will be times we have changed our mind about something that we have promised our children. From our perspective, the situation has changed, and so we just expect them to understand. In fact, we may even get upset with them if they didn't understand. We might say something like: *"Johnny, I know I promised that we would go to the park, but some things came up that I just had to take care of, and now there's not enough time. Maybe next weekend. Okay? . . . Now don't start that crying or you can just forget about the park for a long time to come, young man! Do you understand?"*

Truth be told, Johnny *doesn't* understand and it's *not* okay! However, he is powerless to do anything about it (no choices = frustration). Further, if he feels bad about us breaking our agreement and expresses that bad feeling in tears, we become even more upset, and the situation becomes worse. Now, it's very possible that what came up *was* very important and we had to change our plans. Unfortunately, what we have just unwittingly taught Johnny is that when we tell him something (or make an agreement), we cannot be counted on to do what we say, or even worse, that he isn't as important as "what came up" and that he has no right to feel bad about that fact.

Given that none of this is congruent with our purpose (or what we want to teach), let's look and see how this situation might have been handled more purposefully. First, of course, the fewer times that we break our agreements, the better. When we have made a promise or an agreement with our kids (which they see as the same thing), we might want to think twice about going back on this promise, even if something important *does* come up.

Regardless of what we choose to do, however, we should make sure that we are doing it purposefully and letting our kids in on our thought process. For example, if we do decide to keep our promise to our kids, we should let them know so that they can see the importance of making and keeping agreements. For example, we might say: *"You know, Johnny, I got a call from work today asking if I could come in and work on an account, but I told them that I had already made plans. That's because I believe that whenever we make an agreement in our family, we should do everything in our power to keep it, and I know that when I tell you we will go to the park, that's a promise you want me to keep, right?"*

Of course, Johnny will say *"Right!"* and probably beam with pride that Dad / Mom thinks he is this important. While he is feeling especially good about himself and our relationship, we might want to take the opportunity to tie this to his behavior by saying something like: *"And this is why it's very important that you keep your agreements with Mommy/Daddy. Understand?"* Whether he totally understands or not, he will very probably say "Yes" and this can become a conversation/situation that you can refer to in the future when getting Johnny to "do what you want" will mean keeping his agreements with you.

When we do have to break agreements with our children, we should treat them with the same importance as our child breaking their agreements with us. We might say something like: *"Johnny, I just got a call from the office and they need me to come in and do some work. Unfortunately this means we won't be able to go to the park today and I'm really disappointed about that."* This lets Johnny know what's happening, and that you feel bad about having to break an agreement with him. Therefore, if he responds with tears, you can let him know that you understand how he might be sad about this, given that you are sad, as well. Then you might engage him in some problem-solving by asking him: *"I wonder what we could do (tonight, tomorrow, this weekend, whenever the first opportunity to do something together comes up) to make up for not going to the park?"* This will then give Johnny the chance to focus on the next event, while still conveying the importance of agreements.

When this concept of agreements is paired with giving our children choices, it can become especially powerful. For example, many of the conflicts that arise between parents and kids happen when we, as parents, are wanting them to do something in a timely manner (get dressed, get undressed, come and eat, do their homework, etc.). The problem (from our kid's point of view) is that this almost always interferes with *their* highest purpose in life... having fun, and so they are often less than enthusiastic about doing what we want them to do, when we want them to do it.

Here's how we can combine the concepts of choices and agreements to avoid the conflict and get them to do/be what we want. Let's say that we want our children to come in, wash their hands, and get ready for dinner. Rather than just waiting until it's time for them to eat and then trying to make them stop playing and come in, we could approach them about 15 minutes earlier, and say something like: *"Kids, we are going to be eating soon, would you like to come and clean up now, or play for ten minutes and then come and wash up?"* Of course, they will probably say "play for 10 minutes." However, the good news is that you have given them a choice (which lessens the potential for resistance) and whatever they choose is okay with you. If they do choose to play for ten minutes, you can say: *"Okay, our agreement is that when I tell you ten minutes is up, you will come in and get ready for dinner, right?"* Again, because this lets them return to their mission in life (having fun), they will probably say "yes" without thinking, however, it will also establish an agreement that you can refer to if they balk at coming in at the agreed upon time.

Chances are, however, that there will be less resistance than in the past because you have given them the choice of when to come in, and reinforced the agreement that you have made as a result of that choice. Further, because you have prepared them for what's about to happen (coming in for dinner in approximately ten minutes), they are less likely to be surprised (and frustrated) when you do call them in. However, even if they do start to whine or complain when you call them in, you can now have a conversation about the importance of agreements versus just being obedient. Chances are that you can think of many instances where they would want you to keep your agreements with them (taking them to special events or places) and reminding them of these future situations can go a long way toward motivating them to honor their agreements in the present.

This concept of preparation combined with choices and agreements can be very powerful because kids don't think about time in the same way as adults. As an adult, we are generally making decisions about when to do what based upon our awareness of what needs to be done and how much time we have to do it. Therefore, we often have a "to do" list in our mind and we plan our days around the accomplishment of these tasks. While this makes perfect sense from *our* perspective, our kids are not operating from this point of view. As I have mentioned, their purpose in life is to have fun, and they live very much in the moment. They don't think a lot of the past or the future.

They are primarily concerned with what's

happening now, or more precisely, what's fun now. Understanding this is important because it can help us support our kids in fitting into our schedule. The bottom line is that the more we can prepare our kids for what's about to happen, give them some choices in how they participate, and make clear agreements about how this is going to be handled, the less resistance we will experience. (By the way, we will discuss how these concepts work with the dreaded "bedtime" later in the book.)

Rewards

The third component in this final model revolves around the concept of *rewards.* This is really a very simple concept, however, it can be somewhat controversial. When I am speaking about the value of rewards in getting our kids to do what we want, what I am referring to is making sure the child sees that there is benefit to him or her in choosing to cooperate with us. In my discussions with parents around the country, I find that some parents initially disagree with the idea of rewarding a child for cooperating. They see this idea of tapping into a child's motivation to cooperate by including something that the child wants as "bribery", and have (understandably) resisted this idea, believing instead that their kids should make the choice to do what they are asked because it is "the right thing to do".

I support this concept of "doing the right thing," and believe that it is indeed one of the qualities that most of us as parents would want to teach our children. I think the challenge here is to distinguish between a bribe and a reward.

The dictionary defines a bribe as "something given to someone to induce him/her to act dishonestly" and a reward as "something given or received in recompense for worthy behavior". Clearly, there is a distinction here, and I believe it would serve us as parents to understand this distinction. Since our purpose in teaching our children isn't about inducing them to act dishonestly, but instead to motivate what the dictionary calls "worthy behavior," what we are really talking about when we refer to tapping into their motivation to cooperate are rewards.

Of course, there are many different types of rewards. The good feeling one gets when he or she has "done the right thing" is an internal reward while the money we receive for doing our jobs is an example of an external reward. The point here is that, whether we are going for a warm fuzzy or a cool million, we are all responding to rewards all the time. Our children are no different except that early in their life (say up to about age 12), they are much more concrete than abstract, which means that they are likely to be more aware of (and, thus, motivated by) external rewards than internal rewards. This is why children who often have had trouble learning to be consistent in some area of their life will respond more positively to a progress chart with stars or stickers. They need some tangible representation of their success, and maybe something to work for (a reward) to motivate them to participate in the learning of whatever lesson we are trying to teach.

Does the fact that we pair external rewards with their positive behaviors diminish the learning of those behaviors? Does it teach that they must always "get something" in exchange for being nice, cooperating, or being responsible? Well, it could. If we are using these rewards as ways of manipulating them to do what we want, and there is no intrinsic meaning to them (other than the toy or candy), then this will be part of the lesson which is being taught, i.e. the way to get people to do what you want is to give them something.

Truth is, it depends. What our children learn about rewards (and almost everything else in life) is mostly dependent on (you guessed it) how we interact with them. Do we do things for them just because we love them, and feel good about the act? Do we let them know what we are doing so that they can learn from this? Do we model the qualities of responsibility, compassion, doing the right thing, and talk to our children about how these qualities enhance our experience of life? It is this modeling that will make the biggest impact. In fact, research on the quality of altruism, or the willingness to help another, shows that children who saw their parents participate in altruistic acts were much more likely to display that quality as adults. Remember, children don't always do what we say, they do what we do!

Here is an example of how we might use the concept of rewards (combined with agreements) to motivate our children to cooperate. Let's take one of the more challenging issues that parents and children face all the time . . . homework. Now, I must preface this by acknowledging that my views on the subject of homework are not shared by all parents, and may not be what you believe. I encourage you to take what you find valuable from this discussion, knowing that there are disagreement between professionals and lay people alike about how much homework is "enough" and / or "too much".

As a general rule, I do not believe that lots of homework for children younger than 12 years of age is that helpful in their academic success. I realize this is a controversial topic, and I want you to know that I respect your position of authority as parents. However, I am in agreement with others in the field of education, such as, Dr. Harris Cooper (from the University of Missouri) that suggest the time spent on homework should be no more than ten to twenty minutes for first graders, and ten additional minutes for each successive grade level. Other organizations and associations have suggested similar recommendations: According to statements by the National PTA and the National Education Association (NEA), the following amounts of homework are recommended:

- From kindergarten to third grade, no more than 20 minutes per day.
- From fourth to sixth grade, 20 to 40 minutes per day.
- From seventh to twelfth grade, the recommended amount of time varies according to the type and number of subjects a student is taking. In general, college-bound students receive lengthier and more involved homework than students preparing to enter the workforce immediately after graduation.

Having said this, I also realize that many schools don't follow this guideline, and many parents believe that lots of homework leads to academic success. Further, I am aware that learning to find ways of accomplishing tasks that we may not initially enjoy is part of becoming a successful adult, so let's use the concepts of *choices, agreements* and *rewards* to discuss how this nightly struggle could be handled more successfully.

One reason discussing homework and rewards in the same section makes so much sense, is that getting our kids to do what we want is especially challenging when they seem to have no intrinsic desire to do it (homework, for example). In other words, unless you have one of those rare children that LOVE to sit down and do their assignments, this can be a constant struggle.

As always, if this struggle over homework has been part of your past experience with your child, the first thing to do is speak to the problem in a way where everyone can agree. You might say something like: *"I've been thinking about the arguments that we get into over your homework. I sure wish we could find a way to deal with this without everyone winding up feeling bad. Don't you?"* Remember, nobody likes an argument and so when a situation is approached in this manner, often you can start off in agreement on what needs to change. This is a very important component of successful conflict resolution in any setting.

Next, you focus on your purpose, getting your child to choose to do his or her homework, *and* learning the lesson of how to accomplish a task even when it's not their favorite thing to do (an ability you would probably like them to have as an adult.) Make sense? If so, notice where we have chosen to focus our attention. We are discussing how to get your children to *choose* to do their homework, not on how to *make* them do their homework, or feel bad about not doing their homework (both of which they will resist). This is an important distinction that is reflected in the subtitle to this book (the power and promise of *solution-focused* parenting). You see, whether they do their homework on any given evening is less important than what they are learning from us in the process.

When we focus on the problem (the fact that either their grades will suffer and / or we will be angry with them), we are using fear as the motivating energy. This is problematic because (a) they will resist this approach (and we will have to become increasingly upset in order to enforce our will), or (b) they will be so frightened of our wrath (and / or their failure) that they will do the task and learn that fear is the best motivator to guide their future decisions. While both of these perspectives might "get them to do their homework," chances are neither is congruent with who you want them to be as adults. Let's look and see how this challenging situation might be handled more purposefully from a solution-focused approach.

After you have spoken to what neither of you want (an argument where everyone feels bad), you can acknowledge the fact that doing homework may not be your child's favorite pastime and, yet, it is something that has to be done. This might sound something like. *"Okay, so neither of us likes it when our discussions around homework turn into an argument, and yet, we both know that homework is something that has to be done. Right?"* This statement / question is important because it establishes the fact that a solution must involve getting the homework done. If your child doesn't acknowledge (even if begrudgingly) that this is a true statement, some discussion on the legal requirement of school, and homework as a part of school, might be in order.

Next, you want to engage your children in solving the problem so that the solution isn't about you just trying to force them to obey. The best way to engage a child is to speak to the aspects of life that kids naturally love: i.e. having fun and getting presents (or rewards). For example, you might say something like: *"Let's see if we can tackle this problem in two ways. First, let's see if there is a way to make doing your homework more fun (or at least less miserable) and second, let's see if there is a way you could reward yourself for getting your homework finished."*

While the idea of making homework fun might get less than an enthusiastic response (like they're not convinced that this is possible), I would bet the idea of getting something they want as a reward for doing their homework might spark some interest. If it does, you want to make sure that you include this "spark" in the problem-solving process, because it represents a direct pathway to success, and a signal of your child's internal motivation.

One way of including this spark could be to ask: *"What might you want as a reward for getting your homework done on a regular basis?"* This is important because with this question, you are accomplishing several things. On one level, you are teaching problem-solving skills or how to ensure that important tasks are accomplished, regardless of whether the task itself is that enjoyable. On another, you are giving them choices, and on still another level, you are "asking the expert" (your child) about what might be an effective motivator.

How they respond to this question can be a clue as to how successfully this discussion is progressing, and whether to focus first on short-term, or long-term rewards. For example, if your child says: *"Well, what about if as a reward for getting my homework done, I get to talk on the phone as long as I want?"* (By the way, "talk on the phone" could also be "play my video game", "surf the internet" or any of a number of things that your child would like to do more of). At this point, there is likely to be both some good news and bad news. The good news is that your child is working *with* you (versus *against* you) to find ways to ensure that their homework gets done. This is very good news because it represents a shift in focus from the problem to the solution, and has your child participating in the problem-solving process by actually coming up with ideas. The bad news is that they may be asking for something that doesn't work for you.

Of course, if your child's solution *is* something that you can agree with, you can then discuss how this reward would be put in place and monitored. As you do this, however, keep in mind your goal of continually involving your child in the process by asking them for their suggestions first, and then agreeing with, or modifying their suggestions based upon what works for you. If your child's idea of a reward is *not* something that you can agree with, however, be careful of reacting immediately with *your* resistance to the proposed solution. Like: *"Oh no, we have tried that before, and it only caused more problems"* because your child will just respond with *"No, it didn't"* and you will be right back in the Cycle of Resistance, or power struggle.

Instead, start off by complimenting them on their creativeness and look to see if you might be able to support some aspect of their solution. For example, you might say something like: *"Interesting idea. I tell you what, I would be willing to go along with your solution as long as your (talking on the phone. playing the video game, etc.) doesn't keep you up past your bedtime, go on for longer than an hour (or whatever you are concerned with). If we could make some clear agreement on this, I think we might just have created a solution."* After you and your child hammer out the agreement, you might want to write it down so that there won't be any ambiguity about what was said in the future.

Also, after this agreement has been done, you might want to include another type of reward to further motivate your child in a different way. For example, if she focused on a short-term reward, you might suggest that she also receive something she wants for consistently getting her homework done over a period of time. Of course, the age of your child will play a large role in how long that period is, with longer time periods being more appropriate for older children.

This might sound something like: *"I tell you what, I know that you have really been wanting a (fill in the blank with something that he or she has been wanting, but you have been waiting until a birthday or other holiday to get). If you can do your homework every day for (a certain amount of time with the shortest being twenty-one days), I would be willing to get that for you."* The reason for the twenty-one day minimum period is that it takes twenty-one days of doing something consistently to change a habit.

The important thing to remember here is that often rewards can be the initial motivation to help your children practice behavior that will lead to more valuable lessons. If you consistently pair these more valuable lessons with tangible rewards, you will have your children actively participating in the solution versus struggling with you over the problem. You can then begin to reinforce the internal rewards of self-confidence, pride of accomplishment, the joy of learning, etc. that will serve them well long after the external reward has been forgotten.

Routine

The "R" in this model not only stands for rewards, but also for *routine.* I believe that we as parents consistently underestimate how important the concept of routine is to our children, especially when they are young (say up to the age of twelve). For the most part, kids thrive on routine because it translates into what is known and predictable. It gives them a foundation, or a place of safety and certainty from which to explore the unknown or the unpredictable. If they don't have a sense of routine, they may react to this uncertainty by becoming anxious and, thus, are more likely to act out.

In fact, I'll bet if you think back to some of the times your children were being especially difficult, you will discover that many of these times coincide with a change in their routine. This is why it is important to establish and maintain your children's routines especially around eating and sleeping, because being tired and/or hungry can trigger "acting out" behavior even in the most compliant child. Also, children are generally more willing to do what we want when the thing we are trying to get them to do has been established as part of their daily routine (bedtimes, meals, etc.).

Encouragement

The final concept in this final model of getting kids to do what you want is *encouragement.* This is important because, as we have discussed, one of the most powerful and positive motivators of children is their parent's love and approval. Unfortunately, as we have also discussed, most of us tend to focus our attention on what our children are doing wrong versus their accomplishments.

When we are willing to practice encouraging them "on purpose" (i.e. catching them doing something right and celebrating their accomplishments), we are actually being the sort of loving, supportive adult we want them to become. Our children, in turn, will have less of a tendency to resist this, and are even likely to be drawn to the experience, which can result in their listening and cooperating. This can be a wonderful way to reinforce the qualities we want them to have, while further solidifying our role as supportive guides in our children's lives.

Again, because I believe that it makes my models easier to remember, I like them to spell something meaningful and so this final model spells C.A.R.E.

Choices
Agreements
Rewards/Routine
Encouragement

I'm sure you have heard the statement that people (and especially kids) don't care how much you know until they know how much you care. If our goal is to increase the degree to which our children care how much we know, or see our guidance and advice as valuable information, then we need to pave the way to this appreciative perspective by letting them know how much we care. Not just by saying "I care," but by interacting with them in a way where they feel cared for and loved. *Choices, agreements, rewards,* and *encouragement* are concepts that are designed to accomplish this goal.

Part II

Chapter 9

Real Life!

Let's see where we are in the process of "getting our kids to do what we want" and/or "be who we want." We began with a conceptual discussion of how relating to our children "on purpose," or in a more solution-focused manner, might help us become more influential in their lives (the P.O.W.E.R. model). We then moved into a more specific discussion of how understanding the barriers to our children listening, and then responding to these potential barriers in specific ways could also be helpful (the L.E.A.P.S. model). We then wrapped up our discussion of concepts and tools with the C.A.R.E model, which is designed to work with the other models in helping you become more influential in the lives of your children. We are now about to become even more specific as we discuss situations or problems almost all parents experience in "real life" and see if we can apply these models in creating successful solutions.

I must admit that there is some danger in becoming this specific in a topic so broad as successful parenting, because the solutions suggested here can be seen as "the only right way". So let me be very clear that the ideas and suggestions that we are about to discuss are being offered as "one way" versus "the way". Further, you, as parents or teachers may want to take what you like from these discussions and create your own solutions that more closely match your parenting style, situation, and goals. Remember, the bottom line is to do less of what doesn't work and more of what does.

Okay, before we go any further, I want to speak to those of you who have just skipped to this part of the book because you think this is where the real "meat" is. I know, you may have thought: *"Okay, let's skip the psychobabble and see if this stuff has any merit."* Well, my hope is that you *will* find this section valuable because that is my purpose in writing this book. I would suggest that if you do find value in this section, however, you might choose to go back and read the proceeding material because it should deepen your understanding of and, therefore, your ability to apply what's being recommended here. If you don't find this material as valuable as you would like, just know that it is meant to build upon the concepts discussed earlier which, because they are more general, are meant to be adapted by the reader to their own specific situation.

Bedtime

If there is one problem area where almost all parents would say that they have struggled with their kids, it's around bedtime. For some households, this is like a re-occurring nightmare where kids and parents find themselves caught in a nightly power struggle around what time the kids should go to bed.

On some level, it's easy to see why this would be a problem. Most kids see going to bed as problematic because they are being forced to stop having fun, or at the very least, they are afraid that they might miss something. However, just letting them stay up until they become tired and fall asleep doesn't work because they will invariably not get enough sleep and, thus, be overly tired the next day. Plus, for many parents, this "time after the kids are asleep" is their only "down time," or time to relax and relate to each other as adults.

So, what can be done if your goal is getting your children to go to bed at a time that both gives your kids the rest they need, and provides you with sufficient "adult time"? First, it's important to know what you are wanting and why. In other words, what is your purpose in wanting your kids to go to bed at a certain time? This is important because you always want to have a clear sense of what you want to accomplish (your purpose), and your reasoning behind this decision.

One reason this is important is your kids will very likely want to know *why* they are being asked to stop having fun. If you want them to become adults who seek to understand the reasons behind what they are being asked to do (versus reacting to all demands with blind obedience), you can choose to see this questioning as the good news. This doesn't mean that they will necessarily agree with your reasons, of course, but being clear about your rationale keeps you from falling back into the "because I said so" position, which is guaranteed to meet with either resistance or resentment, or both. In addition, being clear about your purpose will help you focus on the solution (your kids getting the rest they need and you getting your down time) versus the problem (your kids are not doing what you want.) This will go a long way toward avoiding the power struggle, and creating a successful solution.

Further, you will want to have a vision of *how* you would be interacting with them if you were teaching this lesson "on purpose." This, if you remember, is about being clear about what adult qualities you are wanting them to learn as a result of your interacting with them around bedtime. Some of the qualities that come to mind are cooperation, keeping agreements, taking care of themselves (getting enough rest), etc..

Okay, now you are clear about your purpose, what about the "past"? In other words, what has happened in the past, or what patterns or habits have been formed around bedtime, that might be interfering with your purpose? This is important because if these patterns are not addressed, they will continue to interfere with bedtime becoming a successful experience for you and your child.

Children are creatures of habit, and if bedtime in your household has habitually been a time of resistance and struggle, then this will likely continue. Therefore, I suggest that you begin by addressing the problem and the need for change. This could be done by saying something like: *"You know, I've been thinking about how we seem to always get into an argument about bedtime. That really feels crummy to me, and I bet you don't like it either."* Remember, as always, you might say it differently, however, the goal is to raise the subject and define the problem in a way that everyone can agree with.

You might even take some responsibility for the problem (to teach responsibility and to avoid having your children thinking that you are blaming them). You might say something like: *"I think one problem is that I have been springing bedtime on you without warning. You're in the middle of playing, and all of a sudden I tell you it's time to stop and go to bed. What do you think?"* You could then go on to say: *"I think I have an idea about how we could do this differently so that you have more choice about when you go to bed."*

This introduces four concepts discussed earlier that are critical in getting your kids to do what you want in any situation: *choice, agreements, routine,* and *preparation*. I am mentioning them here in our discussion around bedtime, however, we will come back to these concepts many times in this "real life" section because of the powerful role they can play in getting your kids to cooperate while, at the same time, teaching them the qualities that you want them to have as adults. In applying these concepts to bedtime, I'm going to tell you what has worked in my family, but remember, it's the *concepts* that are important, not the specific words or behaviors. This method should be applicable (with some modifications) for children from the ages of around two, up to age eleven or twelve. We will discuss teenagers in a separate chapter.

Okay, remember, we are talking about the problem of bedtime where the kids would probably say that they are being forced to stop having fun and go to bed when they aren't even sleepy. As adults, we would probably say that the kids are being resistant and even argumentative when we are just trying to get them to bed so that they can get the rest they need. Notice in this all-too-familiar scenario, there is no choice, no preparation, and no agreements, and the only thing that routinely happens is a power struggle where everyone ends up feeling angry, hurt, and resentful.

So, how could this be done differently? Well first you need to become clear about the time you want your children to go to sleep. This will vary to some degree, depending on their age, and the time that they will be getting up the next morning. Let's just say for discussion that it's 8:30 p.m. What's important to understand is that this isn't "bedtime," this is the time that you want your children to be falling asleep. There is a difference. For example, if you have decided that 8:30 is when your kids need to go to sleep, then the bedtime routine should start approximately an hour earlier. Why? Choice, preparation, and agreements!

What you want to do is create a routine that prepares them to go to sleep at around 8:30 p.m., and have this routine be repeated every evening. So what do you do? You begin by preparing your kids for what is about to happen, giving them choices, and ensuring that they are making and keeping agreements with you along the way. For example, about 7:30 p.m., you might say *"Kids, it's starting to get late, would you like to go to bed now or play for another 20 minutes?"* Of course, they are going to say play for 20 minutes, but notice what has just happened. You have just prepared them for what's about to happen (versus just "springing" bedtime on them around 8:00 p.m.). You have also given them a choice (go to bed now or play for 20 min.), and set up an agreement where they see the value in cooperating (i.e. they get to play longer).

You then might say *"Okay, I'm willing to set the buzzer and let you play for another 20 minutes if you brush your teeth and put on your pajamas first. Okay?"* The "okay?" is important because you want them to make an agreement with you so that if later they try to change their mind, you can speak to the importance of keeping agreements.

Again, they are much more likely to cooperate with you because they see something in it for them. Plus, the faster they "get ready" (i.e. brush their teeth, put on their pajamas, etc.) the more playtime they will have, which taps into their motivation to get this part of the routine done quickly. By the way, did you notice that there was a reference to a buzzer in the last paragraph? This is important so that there is no argument about how long 20 minutes is, because for your kids, this time will go by in an instant. The "buzzer" can be anything from an alarm clock to the timer on your kitchen stove. Just have it be something that all can hear when it goes off to avoid the argument that it has or hasn't been 20 minutes.

The next potential problem will be what happens when the buzzer goes off. While preparing them for this will take care of some of the resistance, it is understandable that most kids will not be "thrilled" at having to stop playing and go to bed at any time. So, rather than making this "bedtime" (remember your wanting them to go to sleep around 8:30), this becomes "story time". We all know how important it is to read to our kids, *and* how they love it, so we make "story time" part of the transition from "play time" to "bedtime".

This has the advantage of not only beginning to have them engage in a more subdued and quiet activity (listening to you read versus playing) it is something they like. Therefore, at the sound of the buzzer, you move them to the next part of the routine by announcing "story time," and proceeding to one of their bedrooms to read them a short story. If at any time they balk at following the routine, you can remind them about their agreements and give them the choice of being tucked in now, or hearing a story.

After reading to them for ten minutes or so (it's now about 8:00 p.m.) you move to the final phase of the routine by again giving them a choice and making an agreement. You might say something like,
'Okay, would you like me to tuck you in now or would you like to read quietly for a few minutes?" Most kids will choose reading (even if they aren't old enough

they can look at their picture books and call it reading). You can then say: *"All right, you have about ____ minutes (depending on what time you want them to go to sleep) and I will come back in and tuck you in then. Okay?"* Again, you saying "Okay?" is important here because they will almost always say yes, and so, if there is any resistance when you *do* come back to tuck them in, you can speak to the importance of keeping agreements versus making them obey you.

How do you do that? Well, as we discussed earlier, chances are that there have been, and will be times when they want *you* to keep your agreements with *them* (taking them to their favorite play place, park, etc.). You can use this opportunity to help them learn that agreements between family members are very important, and as they honor their agreements with you, you are more likely to keep your agreements with them.

The alternative is a family where parents make promises but don't keep them, and no one can be counted on to do what they say. This can be especially troublesome for a child because so much of their recreation is dependent on adult participation, especially in the area of scheduling and transportation. Therefore, children are often very motivated to live in a home where people keep agreements because this will have a direct effect on what they get to do. Reminding them of this can be a very powerful lesson in the value of one's word, and how important it is to be known as a person who keeps their agreements. Certainly a lesson that will serve them well as adults.

So, let's look at what has happened. Rather than arguing with your kids for thirty minutes to an hour about "doing what they are told," you have created a routine that helps them transition from playing to reading. Given that reading before bed often has the effect of helping your kids wind down, this transition will eventually help them go to sleep. Further, you have done this in a way that gives them choices so that they don't feel so controlled, *and* in a way that allows you to address any problem with a reminder about the importance of keeping agreements.

In short, you have solved the "bedtime" problem by creating a solution that is very congruent with what you want, what is good for them, and even models the qualities that you want them to have as adults. This routine can now become the new "habit," or the way that bedtime is approached each evening, and as such, the repetition factor begins to work in your favor. The challenge, of course, is to do this every evening, at the same time, in pretty much the same way. Otherwise, what will be communicated to your kids is that some nights they will get to stay up later than others, but they will have no control over when that is. This, of course, will have them seeking to influence the outcome by arguing with you, and trying to stay up as late as possible, and you are right back where you started.

If, on the other hand, you begin to practice this solution on a regular basis, your kids will come to expect and accept that this is what's going to happen each night around a certain time (approximately an hour before you want them to be going to sleep.) While it is unlikely that they will necessarily look *forward* to this routine, it *is* likely that they will resist this experience of "bedtime" less than the old one, and, thus, everybody wins.

If, at any point, your children *do* start to argue with you about this new way of handling bedtime, you can again respond in a way that both deals with their resistance, and models the qualities you want them to have as adults. In other words, you can *listen* so that they have a chance to tell you what's important to them, *empathize* with them (i.e. let them know you can understand how they might be disappointed) so that they no longer have to defend their perspective, *ask* them for their ideas about a solution so that you demonstrate respect for their ability to solve problems, and, finally, move in to the *problem-solving* phase in a way that honors what's important to them, as well as, your responsibilities and position as their parent. What is fascinating about using the "LEAP" model (Listen, Empathize, Ask, and Problem-solve) in dealing with our kids is that even when our "solution" is not necessarily what they want to hear, they are able to accept it because they have felt heard and understood.

People can tolerate disagreement. What they cannot tolerate is being tuned out or misunderstood. One of the most interesting comments I have heard from a teenager in describing his relationship with his parents was *"No, we don't always agree on everything, but at least they are willing to listen and try to understand my point of view and that means a lot."* Wouldn't you like this to be the way your children describe their relationship with you?

Making Changes

One more word about change before we move on to the next "real life" problem. I mentioned it to some degree in discussing "bedtime," however, I believe that it deserves more attention because it may be a component that will come up again as we discuss other problematic situations. For many of us, this new solution-focused approach to parenting will be quite a contrast to how we have parented in the past. This is understandable, and yet, if we don't prepare our children for this change, they are likely to be somewhat confused about what's going on. And this confusion could limit the effectiveness of our efforts. For this reason, I am recommending that you talk about the changes as you are making them so that your kids are prepared, and so that they have every opportunity to participate in this new way of relating.

The challenge, of course, is to talk to them in a way that taps into their motivation to value what you are saying. This can often be done by referring to how the old ways of dealing with the problem haven't worked (for you or them). If you remember, we did this in the previous "bedtime" discussion by speaking to how the arguments around bedtime made everyone upset.

Of course, the most powerful way to implement this parenting style is to interact with your children in this manner from the beginning. However, I recognize that most parents reading this book will be doing so because they have had trouble getting their kids to do what they want, and are looking for suggestions about what to change. My hope is that if you fall into this category, you *are* finding this book helpful, and are thinking about the changes you want to make. In order to increase the potential for success, however, it is important, that we take responsibility for setting up these changes in a way that gives everyone concerned an opportunity to understand what is happening, and support this new solution-focused style.

This can be done on a situation-by-situation basis (as outlined in the "bedtime" discussion), or you might consider making somewhat of a blanket statement about what you have found valuable here and how you are going to try dealing with problems differently. For example, you might say something like: *"You know, I have been reading this book on parenting and I think it has some good ideas about how we could solve problems as a family in a more effective way."* Remember, your purpose here is to state this in a way that your kids will support, so you might continue by saying: *"One of the things it says is that, in general, parents don't listen to their kids as much as they should. Would you agree?"* Chances are that 90% of all kids would answer "yes" to this, and so you could add: *"And if parents did listen to what was important to their kids, their kids would be more willing to listen to them. What do you think?"* Again, because almost all kids would *love* to be listened to more, chances are that they would agree with this, as well. You could then go on to talk about giving your kids more choices in creating successful agreements and solutions, versus focusing on who is to blame for the problem.

There are many ways this could be done. I'm just encouraging you to help your family understand this new way of interacting by letting them know what's about to change and why. This way there will be less confusion around and maybe even more support of solving problems in a more purposeful way.

Siblings Fighting

While fights between siblings is a problem faced by almost all multi-child families, there seems to be quite a divergence of opinion on how to handle this situation. I have heard some recommend that you should let your children fight (as long as they are not hurting each other) because this teaches them to deal with conflict later in life. While I do support the idea of children learning to deal with life from within their family, I must tell you that I am not in the "let them fight it out" camp on this one. Now, this doesn't mean that I don't see value in children learning to resolve differences on their own. It just means that when these differences escalate to yelling, name calling, and certainly to physical confrontation, I believe that what is being learned is not congruent with the qualities that I want my kids to have as adults.

I also believe that our jobs as parents is to be aware of what is going on with our kids, and/or between them and their friends, and know when to step in and help them resolve the problem in a mutually-agreeable way. In other words, teach conflict resolution "on purpose" as soon as the situation calls for it. The value of this "early intervention" perspective is that it allows us to address the problem before it escalates into a destructive confrontation.

Of course, in keeping with the theme of this book, we must first become purposeful about how we as parents are dealing with disagreements. Before we start telling our kids how to resolve conflict we must first be sure that we are practicing what we are about to preach. This means that the manner in which the adults in the home deal with disagreements must be congruent with what we want our children to learn about conflict resolution. For remember, our children won't always do what we say, but they *will* do what we do!

Further, having the adults be clear about the value of successful conflict resolution allows us as parents to speak to a family rule when we see a sibling conflict about to get out of hand. We can go to the parties involved and say something like: *"In our family, we don't call each other names, would you like some help in resolving this problem?"* The good news here is whether they say *"yes"* or *"no,"* we can support them in learning a valuable lesson. If they say "yes" we can begin to help them create solutions that model what we want them to do as adults. If they say *"no"* (meaning that they don't want any help in resolving the conflict) we can say: *"Okay, I'm willing to let you two work it out yourselves, however it has to be done so that both of you agree with the solution and without name calling. Can you do that, or do you need some time alone to think about it?"*

If there is one thing most kids don't like, it's having to go be alone and think about what they have done wrong (which is why "time outs" generally don't work and why I have not recommended them as a teaching tool.) Kids mostly want to interact with whoever is bent on having fun (which is generally other kids) and so I use this as a reward for resolving the problem without fighting. The challenge here is to make resolving the conflict more appealing than continuing to struggle with their sibling or friend. The good news is that kids are much better than adults at letting a conflict go if they see that dropping or resolving a problem will get them what they want (which is to have fun.)

The important thing is to catch it early before the hostility becomes too intense or entrenched, and feelings get hurt. If you are able to stop this soon enough and often enough, it will start to become the norm. If, however, there has been a history of fighting between siblings in the home, there is some preliminary work to be done. The problem, of course, is that fighting has become a habitual way of relating, and thus our children will likely find themselves in the middle of an argument almost before they know it. Chances are that neither of the parties enjoy this conflicted way of interacting, but they may see stopping as losing.

Our job as parents (or teachers), therefore, is to (a) raise their awareness about what isn't working, (b) set up the new way of solving problems so that the kids are prepared for the change, and (c) break the habitual tendency to argue or fight in a way that has our kids seeing solving the problem as more attractive than continuing to argue.

You might want to begin to talk about the upcoming change at a time where there isn't a conflict already in progress. This might sound something like, *"Kids, I just wanted to let you know that Dad/Mom and I have been thinking about how our family solves disagreements. Our guess is that nobody likes to fight and it doesn't seem to be producing any long lasting solutions. Anyone disagree?"* Of course, chances are that your kids will not argue for the positive points of arguing or fighting, and so you will at least achieve a tacit agreement. You can then say something like: *"Good! Dad/Mom and I are going to start trying to help you avoid these destructive arguments by paying more attention to when one is about to start and giving you the chance to bypass the fight and move directly to a solution. Sound like a good idea?"*

Again, it isn't necessary here that your kids jump up and down and praise you for your wisdom. What you are doing is preparing the family for change so that when an argument does start (which is guaranteed), you can jump in before it becomes really destructive and say something like: *"Remember the other day (last week, etc.) when I said that we were going to start dealing with disagreements differently? Sounds like this is the beginning of one of those arguments. Would you like for me to help you come to a solution that works for everyone, or would you like to work it out yourselves?"*

This is another one of those times when there is really no wrong answer. If they say *"we want you to help,"* or more likely if they just start blaming the other for the argument, you can say something like: *"I know you don't want to just argue because that just makes everyone feel bad. Let's see if we can put our heads together and create a solution that works for everyone."* Here it is important that we serve as a clarifier versus a referee.

of reframing the situation so that all parties a "place to stand," or a way of understanding what happened without feeling blamed or shamed. This non-judgmental approach is important because what we are *really* going for is a mutually agreed upon solution, not just a more accurate discussion about blame. Plus, I'm sure you can see how the parties involved would be more willing to discuss a solution if they didn't feel they were being blamed or shamed in the process.

If, on the other hand, they say that they would rather work it out for themselves, which really means that they don't want to turn the discussion over to an adult (especially a "parent"), then you can say something similar to what we suggested earlier, such as: *"Okay, I'm willing to let you work it out between yourselves, however, you have to be able to do this without arguing, name-calling, or fighting. Do you think you can do this?"*

This is helpful because it involves both setting down some healthy parameters for how they need to solve the problem, and it even challenges them a little, which often will motivate them to solve the problem successfully just to "show you" that they can. Further, if their attempt to problem-solve *does* disintegrate into an argument, you can jump in and say something like: *"I know that this is hard and it may take some practice, why don't we all take a break and do something else for a short time and see if any ideas about how to solve this come to mind. Let's talk about it in a half hour (or hour) and see if we can reach a solution."* While this "pause" can give all parties a chance to calm down and think about solutions, it is important to set a time to come back and talk again so that it doesn't look like you (as the role model) are trying to sweep problems under the rug. I think you will be amazed at the positive effect a pause in the action can have on arguments that seem to be unresolvable.

The bottom line, of course, is the same as it has been with every other problem and/or solution we have discussed. Always try to interact with your children in a way that teaches them the qualities that you want them to have as adults, and do this by modeling these qualities yourself.

Parenting from the Top of the Mind

As we come to the end of the chapter on "Real Life," this might be a good time to revisit a concept introduced in Chapter One, i.e., the idea that the qualities we want to model and teach (responsibility, compassion, self-confidence, altruism, the ability to work with others, etc.) all come from the upper 80% of our brain. While all of those reactions that we want to avoid (and want our kids to avoid, as well) such as anger, frustration, resentment, stubbornness, resistance, etc., are generated by the lower 20% of the brain or the brainstem.

Plus, given that the focus of this book is on getting our kids to listen and cooperate with us, we now know that when they are in this lower 20%, or the resistant part of their brain, their focus is on resistance. Therefore, before we begin to educate, or inform, we must ensure that we have allowed them to shift from the resistant to the receptive brain (from the brainstem to the neocortex) so that they can hear and process the information we want them to learn.

Of course, this shift is accomplished by our being willing to first hear and understand what's important to them, and then ask a "neocortex question" about the solution and/or the future before we start to problem-solve (the LEAP Model). Further, when they are upset, we must be able to see beyond their brainstem reaction, and know that the person we love is in there somewhere. We need to see them as coming from the fight-or-flight part of the brain, and thus know that they are restricted in their ability to access the clarity, confidence, and creativity necessary to discuss the issue in a "rational" manner. Or, as Neale Donald Walsch puts it:

"True vision is the ability to see in another more than they are showing you."

Chapter 10

Teenagers

Prior to the publication of the first edition of this book in 2002, my kids were ages nine and eleven, and thus I had to start this chapter by acknowledging that, other than working with teenagers as a psychologist, I didn't have "firsthand knowledge" of how these concepts worked for kids over the age of eleven. I did have confidence in the effectiveness of the models and techniques with all ages of kids (or at least with those between the ages of two to twenty) but I also know how important real life experience can be when taking advice from a professional, especially when the advice is about parenting.

Therefore, given that my kids are now ages fourteen and eighteen, I am pleased to report that the material is working as well with my teenage sons as it did when they were younger, and this may be even more important given the fact that many teens and parents experience these years as some off the most difficult.

Of course, one of the things that makes this stage of life so difficult is that teenagers want to be seen as adults, and are frustrated because no one seems willing to treat them this way. However, what if we can change this from the problem to part of the solution? In other words, if we as parents are wanting to support our children in becoming quality adults, and our teenagers are also wanting to be treated as an adult, then we all share at least some common ground. The challenge in getting our teenagers to "do what we want," therefore, is to frame our expectations and goals for them in a way that taps into the key to their cooperation. What is that key? Two words: *respect* and *independence*. The two aspects of family life to which teenagers will react to most dramatically are the times when they feel they (meaning their ideas, priorities, etc.) are not being respected, and when they feel they are being told what to do and/or their independence is being threatened.

This can be especially challenging for parents because, of course, one of our responsibilities is to guide our children through the difficult stages of their lives and in many cases, this will involve disagreeing with their priorities, limiting their independence, and telling them what to do. The question, therefore, becomes this: "Is there a way to fulfill these parental responsibilities and yet limit the problematic "teenager/parent" power struggle that characterizes so many interactions during these volatile years?" Of course, I believe that there is a way, and that it involves many of the concepts that we have already discussed. For example, the concept of interacting with our children based upon the qualities that we want them to learn, would seem to be increasingly important the closer they are to actually becoming adults. Plus, our willingness to interact with them in this "adult" fashion can tap into one of the "keys" to their cooperation, their desire to be seen as an adult, or to have the respect and independence of an adult.

Given that we and our teenagers both want the same thing, it would seem that we could forge an alliance with them based upon this mutual goal. This would likely involve a discussion that went something like: *"So, John, as you become a teenager, my guess is that one of the things you would like is to be able to make more of your own decisions. Am I right?"* Of course, John will more than likely agree with this statement. To which we can respond: *"Great, believe it or not, this is what I want for you as well. In addition, I want to help you make decisions that keep you safe and help you succeed, which I'm sure you want, as well."* (While staying safe and succeeding may have not been John's highest priorities, it's unlikely he will argue against them.)

The good new is that you have just accomplished several things. First, you have built a foundation for discussion that is based upon what is important to your teenager (independence) and further, you have created this foundation on common ground, and begun to form some tentative agreements that revolve around safety and success.

Next, you might want to choose a topic for discussion (say curfew) and put your teenager in the role of parent (which shows respect for his/her ideas.) You might say something like: *"So, John, I'm curious, if you were wanting to set up some guidelines around curfew for your (13 yr. old/15 yr. old, etc.) and your goal was to help them stay safe and make good choices, what would you do?"*

Here the conversation could take several turns. Best-case scenario: your teenager will suggest a curfew policy that works for you, and you can then praise his/her good judgment while creating some agreements around this suggestion. However, what happens if your teenager suggests something unacceptable, such as: *"Well, \Mom/Dad, I believe that as a 13 year old, I should be able to stay out until midnight on week nights and 2 :00 a.m. on the weekends?"* This would likely be unacceptable to you and the temptation, of course, would be to begin to criticize the suggestion, and move back into the "I'm the parent and you will do what I say" response. A response, by the way, that your teenager will almost surely resist.

The challenge here is not to fall into this trap but, instead, continue to interact in a way that supports and demonstrates the qualities you want them to have as an adult, as well as, come to some agreement on the issue at hand. Following this guideline, you might say something like: *"Well, I can understand how you might want that. Sort of like if it were up to me, I would have you in by sundown each evening so that I would know that you are safe. I wonder if we can put our heads together and create an agreement that works for both of us?"*

Chances are your teenager wasn't really expecting you to agree to his/her midnight/2 :00 a.m. proposal, and is willing to come to some agreement that may not be exactly what he/she wants, but is close enough. This ability to compromise and work toward a mutually-acceptable solution (a quality you would probably want him/her to have as an adult) can be supported by your saying something like: *"If we can work this out, I can tell you that it will help me feel better about understanding what is important to you and giving you more independence in the future."* This not only heightens the potential that a mutually-acceptable solution will be reached, it lays the foundation for more of these sort of discussions in the years to come.

Bottom line, when dealing with a teenager, one must be cognizant of many things:

1. This is a confusing time of life where one is expected to not act like a kid, and, at the same time, not have the ability (either legally or cognitively) to make decisions like an adult.
2. During this time in our children's lives, they are learning who they are by first being "not us!" In other words, this is the stage of identity development where kids begin to reject their vision of themselves as a child (and, thus, their dependency on their parents), and begin to see themselves as independent thinkers. The good news is that this is exactly what they need to do to emerge as healthy adults. The bad news is that when our teenagers pull away, and start identifying more and more with their peers, we have a tendency to interpret this as *rejection*. If we are not very purposeful during this volatile time, we will become part of the problem by taking their pulling away personally, and trying to force them back in to the "loving/obedient child" role. This will, of course, only exacerbate their need to pull further away, and a cycle of resistance will result.
3. ***It is during this time of our children's lives that they may need our advice and support the most.*** The problem is that "needing us" is incongruent with

their seeing themselves as independent and, thus, they will be understandably confused. We can ease their confusion and make it easier for them to hear our advice and suggestions if we are willing to let them know that we want to help them become the independent person they are trying so hard to be. Ironically, if they truly believe we are supportive of their transition from child to adult, they may actually open up to us more, discussing more of their life with us, and turning to us more often. Further, it can transform what for most, is a stage of parenting that one hopes to just "survive" into a bridge of life that not only helps those we love become the confident, healthy adults we want, but also lays a foundation for the adult-to-adult relationship that will be the necessary reality for the future. (see page 152 under the short subject: Grown Children: an Oxymoron)

Chapter 11

Short Subjects
(Concepts, not Kids)

This chapter is designed to give you a quick snapshot of how to deal with challenging situations using the models we have discussed so far. As always, the idea is to take what you find valuable, and use it in a way that is congruent with your goals and your style of parenting. The only exception to this rule might be if you have decided that your parenting style is not producing the results you desire, and therefore, you might want to practice some of the previously discussed models until you find one that works for you and your family.

When All Else Fails...!

As we have discussed earlier, this is not about needing to be perfect, just purposeful. We all know that there will be times when we just plain "lose it" and find ourselves doing and / or saying things that are nowhere close to our purpose, or good for our children in any way. The challenge here is to notice what isn't working as soon as possible, and avoid trying to place blame on ourselves or our children. Here, we might want to just practice the Wisdom of Serenity and walk away, gather our thoughts, and return to the situation when we can be the parent we want our children to learn from. Again, this can be both a gift to us (in that we give ourselves the break we need) and our children, in that they learn a way of handling their mistakes and emotions, as well. The bottom line is that if we can be the parent we want to be even 60% of the time, we will be doing a wonderful job, so make sure that you give yourself permission to be human in this challenging process so that your children learn that they can be human (versus *perfect*) themselves.

Hello!!!!! Is Anyone Listening? %$#&@!

One problem I have noticed is how frustrated we, as adults, can become when we walk into a room and start talking to our children and they don't seem to hear what we are saying. In fact, often, they don't even acknowledge our existence. The problem here is that often children are so engrossed in whatever they are doing, they develop a tunnel vision-like focus that blocks out anyone and anything else. As adults, we are more used to "multi-tasking," or doing several things at once, and so we expect this of our children and may even feel insulted and enraged if we are "ignored". Of course the question is: "How is this working for you?"

If it isn't, and your goal is to have your children hear what you have to say, I would encourage you to start by getting their attention. This could be as simple as saying their name and waiting until they look at you before continuing to tell them what you are wanting them to know. With small children, I have found it helpful to ask them to come over to where I am because then I know that I have their full attention. The challenge is to be sure that you are calling them over for rewards and praise, as much as direction and correction, or the experience of your calling their name will begin to take on a sense of dread.

Breaking the Power Struggle by Prescribing the Symptom

We have discussed the problem that the power struggle (or Cycle of Frustration) can cause as we attempt to get our kids to do what we want. A good example (which most parents will face at one time or another) is dealing with a whiney child, or one that is throwing a tantrum. In this type of situation, what normally happens is that the more we try to get them to stop their problematic behavior, the worse it gets, and the more frustrated we become. This is called a *power struggle* because our kids are struggling for power in one way and we are struggling to assert our power in another. Bottom line is that it doesn't work for anyone, no matter who wins.

One way to break this tendency is to step out of the struggle by suggesting that the child do more of whatever they are doing. For example, if the child is laying on the ground screaming and kicking their feet, rather than showing them how upset this makes us (and, therefore, increasing its power), I suggest saying something like: *"Hmmm, Johnny, looks like you are really enjoying that crying. What do you think, wanna do it for two or three more hours?* Generally, he will respond with *"No!"* which is how children respond to everything during this type of experience. The good news is that then you can say something like: *"Really, are you sure you don't want to cry and roll on the floor for an hour or two?"* Again, our kids are likely to respond with *"No!"* and you can say: *"Okay, whatever you want."*

This is generally effective because the child's behavior isn't getting the desired result, and he or she is likely to become somewhat confused. This is okay from my perspective because I would rather my child be somewhat confused about whether he wants to continue crying, versus being determined to win through embarrassing me or wearing me down. Of course, this will require us as parents to allow little Johnny to writhe on the floor (sometimes in public) to convince him that his behavior has no power. What this really means is that we will need to endure the looks (and imagined thoughts) of others to make this work. The good news is that it can be so successful that we will only have to do this a few times. Kids are generally very adaptable creatures. If something isn't working, they will rarely keep doing it. Maybe that's a lesson *we could learn from them!*

Use the Actions of Others as Teachable Moments

As we have discussed, kids are learning every minute of their lives. One way to maximize their learning in a purposeful way is to look for teachable moments where either something is happening between you and them, or behaviors that you and your kids are observing in others that you want them to either emulate or avoid are being witnessed. The best way to support this vicarious learning is to frame what you see in the people you are observing as a result of what *they* have learned, or failed to learn about life.

For example, when you see someone acting in a way that is incongruent with how you want your children to behave, you might say something like: *"Hmmm, looks like that person hasn't learned how to get along with others," I'm sure glad that you have learned this lesson"* or *"I'm sure glad we don't talk to each other that way in our family."* Kids love to be acknowledged for what they have accomplished, and even if they haven't learned this particular lesson as well as you would have liked, your reinforcing these positive traits as what they *have* learned will support their choosing to see themselves in this way and, thus, behave in this manner.

The Magic Phrase for Helping Children Learn from their Mistakes...

As we have discussed, many of us have grown up with our parents pointing out when we did something wrong, and trying to motivate us to correct the problem by either feeling bad about the fact that we did it in the first place, or fearing what would happen if we did it again. Unfortunately, this problem-focused perspective had us either holding an image of ourselves as bad, or fears of being punished as a way to learn and grow and chances are these characteristics (feeling bad and frightened) are not on the list of what you want for your children when they become adults.

As mentioned earlier in the book, a more solution-focused approach to helping children learn from their mistakes is to ask: *"Given what you know now, how would you do that differently?"* This phrase or question is effective because it focuses on the *value* of the solution versus the *pain* (shame, guilt, etc.) of the problem as a motivation to change. It also sends the message that we see our children as intelligent individuals who can come up with quality solutions when given the chance. They therefore begin to see *themselves* that way, and can even surprise us by beginning to look for the learning in their mistakes even before we ask.

Our challenge is to have confidence in their ability to learn versus focusing on our fear of the problem, especially when we are afraid that our children's negative behavior means something about us as parents. Yes, as we all know, often our being upset with our kids has more to do with our fear that their behavior is a negative reflection on us, than whether it is truly harming our children. This is apparent when we react one way to our children acting out at home, and another when we think "somebody's watching". This is problematic because it not only feeds their tendency to use "embarrassing us" as a tool for getting what they want, it teaches our kids that the way to manipulate people is to embarrass them.

So, next time your children make a mistake, rather than ensuring that they feel bad about the problem, focus instead on the solution, and ask *"Given what you have learned, what would you do differently next time?"* I'll bet you will be amazed at the results.

"You are making me so angry! Do you *want* me to hurt you to make you behave?"

One of the problems I have found with parenting from a problem-focused perspective, is that it seems we must get really upset before our kids pay any attention to us. This is a problem because 1) they learn not to pay attention until we start yelling and 2) we wind up stressing ourselves out on a regular basis in order to have any influence with our kids.

Given that we will be correcting our children for a significant part of their lives, I would suggest that we learn to do this in a way that doesn't require that we become furious to be effective. One way to do this is to create agreements with our kids about how they will behave with rewards for their keeping their agreements, and mutually-agreed upon consequences if they don't. This way, when your kids behave the way they have agreed to, they get rewarded, and when they don't, *they* feel bad because of the agreed-upon consequences. In fact, rather than the problem being that you were upset, you can even empathize with their sadness and let them know that you would love to help them do it differently next time.

Back-talk as a symptom of the relationship, or...
"Don't you talk that way to me. young man!"

One problem almost all of us will face at one time or another in our role as parents is when our kids choose to deal with a problem by "talking back", or speaking to us in a rude and disrespectful way. The common reaction to this problem is for us to talk to *them* in a rude and disrespectful way, and try to frighten them into changing. The reason this rarely works long-term is that if our kids have any intelligence at all, they see that we are being somewhat hypocritical in our instruction. In other words, ***being disrespectful to our children to teach them to respect us is generally a bad idea.***

So what can we do? Certainly, not ignore it and hope it goes away. In fact, I suggest that the first time our children try the "back-talk" approach to problem-solving, that we look at them as if they have just said something totally out of character, and ask them some questions. For example, if in the middle of some disagreement your child says *"I hate you! You're a bad Mommy!"* rather than the *"Don't you talk that way to me, young man!"* response (which only shows that the barb had its intended affect) I would encourage you to look at him and ask *"Really? You think I'm a bad Mommy? . . . Wow, that must be sad to think you have a bad mommy. I am sure glad that I don't hate you or think that you're a bad son."*

He will likely be somewhat confused by this response, and so you might follow up with: *"I bet you are glad that we don't yell at each other the way we have seen some Mommies and kids do. Would you like to talk about what is upsetting you?"* Using this approach, you are accomplishing several things: 1) You are making his "being upset" about him versus you, and 2) You are interacting with him in a way that says you don't really see him as a person who talks this way to those he loves. This will be a perspective that is hard to argue with. Finally, you are modeling the sort of behavior that you would like him to be able to use with others, which is about questioning the attack versus defending yourself.

If this is not the first time your children have talked to you in this manner, we must take a different approach. The challenge is to see the behavior as a symptom of what isn't working in your relationship with your child versus what's wrong with him or her.

We must begin by recognizing that babies are not born with this tendency and thus, this is a learned response. *Where* he learned to talk to you in this way will be an important determinant of how you address the problem. For example, if this way of speaking is similar to how you talk to him, or how he has seen the adults in the family talk to each other, then it will be important for you to take responsibility for changing your part of this dysfunctional dynamic first.

Remember, our children see us as the ones with all the power and, therefore, they will naturally emulate how we interact with them and others. Further, if we continue to speak to our children, or the other adults in the family in this disrespectful manner, our attempts to get them to treat us with respect will seem incongruent and even hypocritical.

Once we have decided to change the way we interact with our children (and others), then it would be a good idea to talk to our kids about this change, and make some *agreements* about how our family deals with *disagreements*. After this new way of interacting is established, you can use the technique described above to reinforce the change.

The bottom line is that you want to see the problem (your child being disrespectful) as an aberration, or something totally out of character. This way, rather than getting in to a power struggle (which you can surely win, but the cost will be you getting upset and your child feeling like a loser) you can respond from a position of shock and confusion. In fact, often the best response is to just stare incredulously at the child (as if they just said something in "Martian") and ask *"What was that?"* This has the effect of turning the focus on their problematic response in a way that is very hard for them to defend. Then you can follow what will most likely be a very awkward silence with some of the phrases we discussed earlier.

Kids and Restaurants

One of the challenges that most parents will face is dealing with the problems kids create in restaurants (or as our children might say, the problems restaurants create for kids.) This generally happens when the family is waiting for the food, or the check, or when our little ones are bored, and are looking for something to do. This situation can be handled in two ways. First, kids need to know beforehand if they are expected to behave in a specific way in a specific situation. Generally, going out to dinner is a different experience than having dinner at home, and many parents seem to think kids will just naturally know this and behave accordingly.

When this doesn't happen (which is almost guaranteed), parents have a tendency to be embarrassed (as if their children's behavior is a direct reflection on them) and try to "make" the kids behave. This, of course, only produces more problems in the form of a power struggle or a shaming experience for the kids, neither of which models or teaches them the qualities you want them to have as adults.

So, what to do? As mentioned earlier, first make sure that kids know what is expected of them in this particular situation. You might want to spend a few minutes discussing the difference between how we behave during dinner at home, and how we want to be at a restaurant. You might make some agreements about this and give them something to work for so that they will have an internal motivation to practice the behavior you have outlined. In fact, you might want to practice this behavior with a "pretend trip to a restaurant." Choose someone to play the role of the waiter (preferably an adult), and give your children the opportunity to "learn by doing" (which, by the way, is the most effective way to learn).

Second, make sure that you are aware of the difference between a child and adult in terms of attention span.

To expect a child to sit quietly and engage in polite small talk is generally a recipe for disaster. Instead, have something to occupy their little minds and imaginations. Things like coloring books, puzzle books and even game boys (with the sound off) can keep them occupied very nicely during those times when either the food has not arrived or everyone is finished and waiting for the check. You might even have your child pick out "special books" that are only looked at in restaurants to make the event seem even more of a treat. By the way, this can apply to almost any similar situation, such as, car trips, waiting in the airport, visits to the doctor and dentist, etc. The overall idea is to engage the child in material that is age-appropriate and enjoyable so that the natural boredom that most children have when they are not "doing anything" doesn't become a problem.

In general, this is about not expecting kids to have the same priorities that you do in any given situation. Remember, their mission in life is to have fun. The more you tap into this natural motivation and help them have fun in a way that also works for you, the happier everyone will be.

"Grown Children"...An Oxymoron

The tendency for us as parents to see our offspring as our "children" (no matter what their age) is, in my opinion, responsible for a large majority of conflict in families with "grown children". Of course, this doesn't mean that we can't hold them and love them as we did when they were a child (if this is, indeed, what they need and/or want). It just means that seeing them as "children" and therefore "one down" on the ladder of authority, or seeing our role as advising them on what they should and shouldn't do almost always causes misunderstanding and conflict. Further, this position of "father/mother knows best" is often incongruent with what we want for them, i.e. their becoming independent adults.

I would encourage you instead, to treat them as who you want them to be (as well as who they really are), adults, who must make their own decisions, and sometimes learn from their own mistakes. This, of course, means giving up our position as the "wise ones" and creating a more egalitarian relationship with our "grown children" which, for some parents, is hard to do. While this is understandable because it means changing well established relationship patterns, I believe that the benefits of reduced conflict and increased love and appreciation will be well worth the effort. And who knows, if we are willing to step back and let our "grown children" make their own decisions, it may, ironically, increase the likelihood that they will come and ask us for our opinion.

The "Rewind" Solution

In my work with parents (and in my experiences with my own children) I find that most problems don't "just happen," but instead follow a pattern of gradual escalation. In other words, our kids will do or say something that we don't like (maybe running in the house, or playing a bit too rough, not paying much attention to what we are saying, etc.), but rather than address the problem, we just continue to let it go until it gets to the point where something bad happens or it's just finally driving us crazy! Then we jump in with all of our built-up frustration and attempt to deal with the situation. While this is understandable, I'm going to suggest that this method of dealing with problems may not be working for us, or our kids.

What I propose, instead, is to first try to set up agreements as early as possible so that everyone knows what is agreed-upon behavior. Second, monitor your kids so that when the behavior starts to go beyond these boundaries (which is guaranteed), you can catch it early and thus help your kids make choices that are more congruent with the sort of family situation that you want to create, and the type of adults you want them to become. However when, for whatever reason, we miss this "catch and correct" opportunity, I think we can still learn from a situation gone wrong by what I call the "rewind solution". Simply put, the "rewind solution" involves looking back over the time that lead up to the problem to see where it began, and how we as parents might want to deal with it differently next time.

For example, let's imagine that your kid's rough behavior escalates into a fight, or someone getting hurt. Often, the drama of such an outcome, coupled with your being upset, tends to have everyone focused on the problematic event, and "who's to blame" becomes the game everyone seems to start playing. Unfortunately, this only has the parties involved working hard at abdicating responsibility, and does little to ensure that this sort of problem won't happen again.

What if instead, after the fight has been stopped and / or the hurt person tended to, you begin to "rewind" the "video tape" that lead up to this situation. That is, you begin to let your mind review the events that lead up to the problem in order to find a place where you might have intervened so that you have some idea about what you want to do differently next time.

For example, you might remember that their behavior seemed rough to you earlier, and either you didn't say anything or (more likely) you did say something, but your kids didn't change how they were playing or interacting. With this new awareness, you might say something like: *"You know kids, I was concerned that something like this was going to happen when I noticed how rough you were playing earlier. I now wish that I had given you the chance to change how you were playing, or choose a game that wasn't so rough. It's not okay that you two got into a fight and/or that someone got hurt. So, I tell you what, if you two think that you can play together in a way that doesn't end in a fight or someone getting hurt, then I will go ahead and let you play. However, if I see this start to happen again, I am going to step in and give you the choice of changing the game or playing separately. Okay?"* They will probably respond with a begrudging "Okay" and you can repeat the agreement so that all understand what is going to change.

As I have said repeatedly, the specific words

that you choose here aren't important. What is important is that you have used your awareness of what led up to the problem as good information, and have informed your children of your intent to make different choices in the future. Further, the focus isn't on who's to blame, but how you as a family can ensure that this doesn't happen again.

Also, notice how the concepts of choices and agreements have been worked into the discussion. Your children have been given the opportunity to see the situation from your perspective, and now they know that, in the future, when you step in (which is probably guaranteed) they will have the chance to choose how they handle the situation. They can either change the game or play separately. If, in the future, they balk at this solution, you can remind them of their agreement and ask them if they see any other way to solve the problem. Regardless of what they choose, the cycle of escalation has been interrupted, and the potential for a more purposeful outcome has been greatly enhanced.

The important thing to remember here is that almost every negative event is preceded by a string of negative events, and the earlier you can intercede (or better yet, give your kids the opportunity to intercede on their own behalf), the more influential you can become in preventing problems from getting out of hand.

Chapter 12

Conclusion

My sense is that by now you know what the title of the book **"How to Get Kids To Do What We Want"** is all about. It's about interacting with our children in such a way that reduces their resistance to what we have to say while, at the same time, teaching them the qualities that we want them to have as adults. Further, my hope is that you have found the concepts behind the title and the subtitle ("The Power and Promise of Solution-Focused Parenting") to be helpful and meaningful in reaching your goal of becoming a more effective parent, guardian, or teacher in the lives of your children.

As I have said throughout, my goal in writing this book is to help you become more influential in your children's lives. I hope I have also conveyed my desire for you to take from this book what you find valuable and adapt it to your personality and your unique style of parenting or teaching.

Finally, let me encourage you to be kind to yourself as you strive to incorporate these concepts into the way you interact with your children. It's not about being perfect, it's about being purposeful. As mentioned earlier, if we can become a more "purposeful parent" even 60% of the time, we will have given our children and ourselves a priceless gift. In fact, as we have discussed, in being purposeful, we can even use our mistakes as ways of teaching those we love how to learn from the times when *they* may say, or do something that is incongruent with who they really are,

One of my favorite professors, Dr. Walt Cubberly, once said: *"Never try to become a perfect parent. It doesn't give our children any thing to be better than."* Therefore, here's to a life of interacting with our children in a way that allows them to both cooperate more (do what we want) and, more importantly, become the intelligent, responsible, honest, compassionate, successful, trustworthy adults we want them to be. And, if we do our best, and our children do even better with their children, and their children do even better with their children, who knows what sort of world could be created? Sort of a nice legacy, don't you think?

Appendix

About the Author

Bill Crawford, Ph.D. is a psychologist, organizational consultant, corporate trainer, and professional speaker currently residing with his wife and two sons in Houston, Texas. He holds a Bachelor's degree in Music Education, and both Master's and Doctoral degrees in Counseling Psychology from the University of Houston. Over the past 25 years, Dr. Crawford has created over 3200 presentations for such organizations as Sprint, JPMorgan / Chase, Shell, The Texas Medical Center, and professional associations nationwide. Dr. Crawford has a unique perspective on life and success that he shares with such humor and energy that he is constantly referred to as the "Steve Martin" of psychologists. In addition, he has been quoted as an expert in such diverse publications as The New York Times, Entrepreneur, The Chicago Tribune, Self Magazine, Investor's Business Daily, Cosmopolitan, The Dallas Morning News, and Working Mother Magazine, and he has hosted two PBS specials that have been seen by over 15 million people nationwide.

Keynotes, Trainings, & Other Presentations

If you have enjoyed the material in this book and believe that it would be valuable for others in your organization, the keynote or training based upon this book is entitled ***How To Get Kids to do What You Want!*** Dr. Crawford is also known for his ability to impact audiences on several other topics. The most popular of these are listed below:

Life fom the Top of the Mind

All Stressed Up & Nowhere To Go!

From Chaos to Calm: Dealing with Difficult People vs. Them Dealing with You!

Getting Others to Get It: Ensuring That What You Say is Heard and Acted Upon.

For more information, please contact Dr. Crawford at:
1-888-530-8550
or visit his website at:
www.billcphd.com

Made in the USA
Las Vegas, NV
18 April 2024

88848506R00094